PRAISE FOR MO*

"*More Money Now* goes where mos~~...~~ ~~...~~ don't—Nicole Victoria actually provides actionable insights and monetary suggestions, while tackling the taboo subject of subconscious beliefs surrounding money. I believe this book is going to help people from every walk of life."

—**Alexandra Fasulo**, author of *Freelance Your Way to Freedom*

"In a world filled with finance bros and out-of-touch academics, Nicole's self-made story and empathetic approach cuts through the noise. Instead of wagging a finger from an ivory tower, Nicole gets right at the heart of our failed relationship with money. I had a 'mind blown' moment when she described how our money mindset is shaped by the age of seven and rarely ever relearned. Slapping a budget-Band-Aid on that innate issue rarely results in lasting improvement. If you're ready to change your relationship with money and start building serious wealth, *More Money Now* will show you how."

—**Jeremy Schneider**, retired at 36, founder of Personal Finance Club

"This book is an eye opener. *More Money Now* will absolutely change your psychology around money. In a world of job insecurity and high inflation, the information presented in this book is important now more than ever. It's filled with practical strategies to make meaningful progress towards securing the financial future of you and your loved ones."

—**Jim Chuong**, Canadian Millionaire Coach

MORE
MONEY
NOW

MORE
MONEY
NOW

A Millennial's Guide
to Financial Freedom
and Security

NICOLE VICTORIA

mango
PUBLISHING
CORAL GABLES

For permission requests, please contact the publisher at:
Mango Publishing Group
2850 S Douglas Road, 4th Floor
Coral Gables, FL 33134 USA
info@mango.bz

For special orders, quantity sales, course adoptions and corporate sales, please email the publisher at sales@mango.bz. For trade and wholesale sales, please contact Ingram Publisher Services at customer.service@ingramcontent.com or +1.800.509.4887.

More Money Now: A Millennial's Guide to Financial Freedom and Security

Library of Congress Cataloging-in-Publication number: 2022937191
ISBN: (p) 978-1-64250-948-9 (e) 978-1-64250-951-9
BISAC category code BUS050030, BUSINESS & ECONOMICS / Personal Finance / Money Management

Printed in the United States of America

For my husband Justin, and children Liam and Zachary. Even though I did not come from a wealthy family, a wealthy family will come from me.

CONTENTS

Introduction   10

CHAPTER 1
How Did We Get Here?   21

CHAPTER 2
A Budget Won't Solve Your Problems   35

CHAPTER 3
If Not a Budget, Then What?   50

CHAPTER 4
Money Mindset   57

CHAPTER 5
Basic Money Rules   76

CHAPTER 6
Are You Asking Broke Questions?   127

CHAPTER 7
Getting Your Partner on Board with Your Goals   170

CHAPTER 8
Saving Is Only Part of The Battle   182

CHAPTER 9

Grow Your Money in the Stock Market   193

CHAPTER 10

Final Thoughts   227

Glossary of Terms   233

Acknowledgments   239

About the Author   241

INTRODUCTION

HOW TO USE THIS BOOK

Depending on where you're at in your life right now, when you think of feeling secure with your money, it might seem like an impossible task.

Maybe for you, money has always seemed complicated. Maybe it was something you were brought up to believe was a taboo topic, something you didn't discuss with family or friends. Maybe you believe that because you're not good with math, you absolutely couldn't be good with money.

Maybe you are stuck in the fixed mindset that where you are right now has to be where you remain forever. That where you came from dictates where you get to go in life. That if you didn't come from money or marry into money, you are forever going to be someone who struggles with money because *that's just the way life is.*

Maybe you have debt (hello student loans and credit cards), and you feel like you'll always be playing catch-up. Maybe you've tried to get help before, tried to budget, followed traditional advice, but *it just doesn't work for you.* Maybe you're stressed, overwhelmed, and feeling stuck because you don't know where things went wrong.

I've been in many of these places myself. I grew up in a lower middle-class household with no one to teach me about money, let alone saving and investing. Personal finance wasn't taught in school or at home, or so I thought. The crazy thing is, even if you don't believe you were taught about money, you actually were. You were taught by the things you saw and experienced, what you heard your parents or caregivers say and do, and what your life experiences were as a child. Without someone there to truly guide us on the best ways to do things, our financial problems can fester and grow.

Did you realize that by the time you were seven years old, you'd already created the internal money rules and scripts you'd use to run your entire life? And if you don't take the time to relearn and update them, at twenty, thirty, forty, and fifty years old, those same rules are used to make your financial decisions around spending, saving, debt, and more? Your seven-year-old self, who believed in the tooth fairy, created the rules you could be using today to make decisions that can fundamentally impact your entire life. Scary shit, right?

By the age of ten, I was taught (unintentionally) that credit cards were emergency funds and that if you saved money, you were just a different breed of person. That wealthier family members just got lucky, and people who saved instead of spending all their dollars were cheap. That success was how much shit you owned, and the more expensive your car, the better off you were. I saw my family struggle with money, and I told myself, "That isn't going to be me." I wanted so desperately to "get lucky," like the other people who had built wealth—so I did what most people do in search of a better life: I went to university so I could become more educated, get a better and higher-paying job, and then get all the wealth and success that was supposed to come along with it.

Instead, I ended up graduating with $40,000 in student loan debt—a lot of which I'd spent on clothes and margaritas—and working a job that didn't bring the bags of cash I was promised. And I know I'm not alone in the belief (and misconception) that success with money is as easy as signing up for a four-year degree at any post-secondary institution—regardless of what your major is, and taking out student loans to pay for it (because of course you'll be financially successful after graduation, and won't have any trouble paying those loans back). Well, suffice it to say that was a crock of shit—because there I was, bright-eyed and bushy-tailed, graduating with a business degree, in my "cushy" corporate job, not feeling any further ahead financially then I was before my foray into tens of thousands of dollars of debt.

Like many of you reading this, I was at that age where I wanted to get married, buy a house, and feel financially stable enough for kids— *maybe even get to say yes to guac at a restaurant without thinking about the cost*—but I was living from paycheck to paycheck with $0 in savings, and I had no idea how I was going to be able to turn it around. I had no idea what to do, because the roadmap to success I had been sold in high school actually just turned out to be a debt trap.

The "rules" I had been taught about money, success, and wealth weren't working for me. I thought maybe the problem was that I just didn't make enough money, yet. I thought the corporate job was the golden ticket, but maybe I just needed a promotion. But when I looked around at the people who had the job title above mine, they seemed to be in a similar situation. Maybe some of them had experienced the wedding, bought the house, and had the kids, but they weren't more financially stable or secure. They were stressed and living under mounting piles of debt to keep up with their "dream life."

So I thought to myself, *Okay, Nicole, you're a data-driven person—let's get down to the studies and find out exactly what is going on here.* I wanted to understand why, if these people were following the life path we'd all been told to follow, they were all seemingly struggling so much financially.

That's when I found these shocking statistics:

- 79 percent of consumers who have a budget fail to stick to it.[1]

- 54 percent of consumers live paycheck to paycheck.[2]

- 80 percent of Americans are in debt.[3]

- 40 percent of Americans cannot afford a four-hundred-dollar un-expected expense.[4]

- 64 percent of Americans don't have enough money to retire.[5]

One of the most shocking statistics I found was a decline in happiness in the US:

- In 2012, 50 percent more Americans reported they were "not too happy" than was reported in the 1990s, and by 2016–17, adults and adolescents reported even less happiness than in the 2000s.[6]

Everyone I'd witnessed seemed to be doing what they were told to do, but that traditional advice wasn't working.

---

1   cnbc.com/2019/12/26/consumers-overspend-by-7400-a-year-here-are-weekly-trouble-spots.html.

2   prnewswire.com/news-releases/nearly-40-percent-of-americans-with-annual-incomes-over-100-000-live-paycheck-to-paycheck-301312281.html

3   cnbc.com/2015/07/29/eight-in-10-americans-are-in-debt.html

4   abcnews.go.com/US/10-americans-struggle-cover-400-emergency-expense-federal/story?id=63253846

5   ca.style.yahoo.com/survey-finds-42-americans-retire-100701878.html

6   worldhappiness.report/ed/2019/the-sad-state-of-happiness-in-the-united-states-and-the-role-of-digital-media/

Traditional advice tells you to:

- **Take out student loans to go to school because they are considered *good debt* and an investment in your future.**

  The average student in America graduates with $38,792 in debt, which is an all-time high.[7] Now society has people stretching the meaning behind this advice to justify taking out $200,000 in student loans to get a job that pays $40,000 annually, as, for instance, when students declare a low-yielding major at an expensive out-of-state-university, change majors multiple times in their college career, or have hopes of high incomes (based on crafty marketing efforts by the school) when the actual job prospects don't support it—like the "become a famous writer" or "celebrity chef" promises where the hourly starting wages run between nothing and fifteen dollars per hour, but the programs run tens to hundreds of thousands of dollars.

Societally, the emphasis has been put on just going to school without ever thinking about the return on that investment. (Are you actually going to make your money back, and if so, how long will that take?) It's like everyone stopped looking at these things with logic because this "rule" has become so ingrained into our culture. Who decides that something is a good investment without ever looking at the cost and how much you can get back? Society has put an emphasis on going to the most prestigious college we can get into, instead of looking at the one that can get us closest to our dream life. This means thinking about the cost and how you're going to pay for it—*not jumping in with eyes wide shut*. It's important to think about what you're giving up by going there

---

7   federalreserve.gov/publications/2021-economic-well-being-of-us-households-in-2020-student-loans.htm

because *everything is a tradeoff*. When we say yes to something, we'll have to say no to something else.

And taking this path is having major repercussions: 77 percent of millennials report having financial anxiety, which is bleeding over into other areas of their life. Based on my anecdotal work with women on their finances, this has impacted everything from their mental health to their physical health and relationships.[8]

People are more stressed, feeling like they're behind the ball and have no way to get around it. Add in stagnant wages and increasing housing prices, and it's pretty clear that conventional wisdom has actively led people into the life they were trying to get away from by going to school. It's a running joke: I went to school to get a job, and now I have to get a job to pay for my school.

- **Buy a new car when you graduate to showcase your success. You *deserve* it.**
The average cost of a new car: $41,000 plus the cost of financing.[9] Now, let's start off with the fact that cars are notoriously the worst place to put your money. I don't care that in your accounting class, they were classified as an asset. They're truly a liability, because they take money from you every month and lose value to the tune of 40 to 50 percent in the first five years.[10] That means if you bought a vehicle for $30,000 when you graduated, within five years it could be worth only $15,000. To top it off, not only are new grads starting off with debt from school, now they're piling on more debt with a new car before they've even earned their first paycheck. "I deserve it" has become a catch-all

---

8   cnbc.com/2020/06/25/young-people-stressed-all-over-world-but-dont-blame-coronavirus.html

9   finance.yahoo.com/news/average-new-car-price-hits-record-41000-130015214.html

10 birchwoodcredit.com/blog/how-much-does-a-car-depreciate/

phrase people use in the name of "self-care." In reality, taking care of your finances is the ultimate form of self-love.

- **Get married and have the lavish wedding of your dreams—treat yourself, you deserve it!**
Over 28 percent of Americans go into debt for their weddings—and we're not just talking a couple thousand dollars. The average cost of a wedding has ballooned to over $30,000. You may be reading that and thinking, *Okay, Nicole, 28 percent going into debt isn't that much*, but this is where we need to remember that everything in life has an opportunity or tradeoff cost. If these couples are choosing to spend their $30,000-plus here, they're not spending it (saving it, paying off debt with it, investing it, etc.) somewhere else. The craziest thing about this is that most couples invite so many guests, they are so rushed trying to speak with and thank all the people they invited on the day of the wedding that they don't even get to enjoy it.

Not to mention the fact that couples who go into debt for their weddings are more likely to consider divorce—almost half of all newlywed couples cited considering separation due to money issues.[11]

Now, this raises the question (and it is kind of a chicken-or-the-egg scenario): Is it the wedding debt that spurs the stress that has 47 percent of couples thinking about cutting ties, or is it the potential lack of financial literacy and education that caused them to take on the financial burden of wedding debt in the first place—meaning there are likely to be further money issues within the marriage? Either way, it's important to consider how having your "dream day" could end up costing you your "dream life."

---

11 businessinsider.com/couples-go-into-wedding-debt-more-likely-to-consider-divorce-2019-7

- **Buy your dream house, spending as much as the bank's loan pre-approval will allow.**

  The average cost of a home in the US is $344,000,[12] which has been steadily rising over the past decade. I sold real estate for six years (I've parked my license now), and something that I saw repeatedly was young couples stretching their last dollar to buy their dream house. They focused on spending as much as the bank said they could spend with their pre-approval, instead of crunching their own numbers and considering the lifestyle they wanted to lead. The banks look at a variety of factors when coming up with your approval amount, none of which account for the kind of life you want to live. They don't care about how you're going to afford daycare for kids you may have in the future; they don't ask if you like to travel, or have an active social life (which usually involves spending money of some sort). And these young couples, wide-eyed and dreaming, sometimes max out their pre-approval without a second thought—because *the bank said we could afford it.*

- **Keep up with the Joneses with "buy now, pay later."**

  We're told that "buy now, pay later" is an incredible tool that frees us from having to delay satisfaction. We can have everything we ever wanted, without having to work for it first. We'll get it now, and then pay it back (plus interest), over the next few months, or years. The average family now has over six thousand dollars in credit card debt.[13]

When all is said and done, by the time most of us are in our twenties, the average person has racked up $23,872 in debt, and this number jumps to $62,658 in our thirties.[14] The scariest thing about these numbers is that

---

12   zillow.com/home-values/

13   valuepenguin.com/average-credit-card-debt

14   businessinsider.com/personal-finance/average-american-debt

we have never been shown the effective ways to pay it down: One in five millennials with debt expects to die without paying it off.[15]

To make matters worse, no one tells you that the best time to start building wealth is in your twenties. In your twenties, you have the power of time on your side, so you can build more wealth with less financial input (less of your actual money) because you can give it more time to grow.

However, when you tell anyone you're struggling, they tell you it's a simple math problem and that you just need to create a budget, as if a budget is the magic-pill solution to all your problems. They tell you things should be adding up, and if they're not—*you're doing something wrong.* What they don't tell you is that budgeting has been proven to not work for 79 percent of people who have tried it.[16] So if we are being told the only solution to our money problems is to budget, but budgets are proven to fail, we have been given advice that truly sets us up for serious financial problems in our lives.

So here we are—young, successful, and drowning in debt—with traditional advice failing us. This, in and of itself, creates an inner turmoil and pushes many of us into a quarter-life crisis. Trust me, I've been there. My early twenties turned into "Who am I? Why am I here? What's the freaking point of any of this?" *real quick* when I realized this dilemma. If the rules I had been sold about life and money got me a life I didn't want, then it was up to me to rewrite the rules.

I decided there had to be a better way. I knew there were people who had done what I wanted to do, but how? I got gritty. I took radical

---

15 cnbc.com/2019/01/08/1-in-5-millennials-with-debt-expect-to-die-without-ever-paying-it-off.html
16 cnbc.com/2019/12/26/consumers-overspend-by-7400-a-year-here-are-weekly-trouble-spots.html

responsibility. I learned everything I could about money, personal finance, real estate, and investing.

Using this newfound knowledge, I was able to:

- Pay off $40,000 of debt in eighteen months

- Pay for my wedding in cash

- Save my first $100,000 by twenty-five

- Buy my dream home

- Become financially stable enough for kids

- Build a $500,000 net worth in my twenties

- Grow that net worth to over $1,000,000 at thirty

If I had kept following the traditional path— using the societal advice that's pushed on us—I wouldn't be where I am today. That's why I've written this book.

I know that what I've accomplished seems like an outlier, but the process is much simpler than you think when you learn the money rules I've outlined in this book, based on my own personal finance journey. The advice that worked for our parents won't work for us. Times have changed, and our reluctance to find another way is why more and more people are unhappy and in debt.

To be good with money and to build wealth:

- You don't need to be good at math

- You don't need to be born rich

- You don't need a six-figure salary

By following a few simple steps, principles, and rules, you can manage your money without a budget, without giving up everything you love, and without restriction. You can build wealth. You can have a savings account. You can invest. Remember: investing isn't just for the rich—it's how you get rich and build financial security.

All of this brings me to my book's promise—what I promise you are going to get out of reading and committing yourself to the processes outlined in this book. **I promise this book is going to teach you how to manage your finances without a budget and help you feel empowered with your money.** Without restriction. Without giving up everything you love. Without the outdated advice that just doesn't work.

You need this book—not because I want you to buy it, but because this process has changed my life, and I've watched it change the lives of thousands of others. Now it has the opportunity to change yours too. If we want something different, we must do something different. Following traditional and average advice is going to get you a traditional and average life, and the average person is in debt, unhappy, and working a job they hate. That doesn't have to be you. The first step is learning there is another way, and I'm here to teach it to you.

Are you freaking ready? Let's go!

CHAPTER 1

HOW DID WE GET **HERE**?

We know that traditional advice isn't working for today's generation, but how did we get here? Whether you're a recent college grad with a mountain of student loan debt and no foreseeable student loan forgiveness in sight, or a newlywed who's come down from the magical high of her special night—you have taken the first step in changing your financial situation and going after your dream life. That's a huge step, so kudos to you! Part of moving forward is first assessing where you've come from, which may require asking ourselves, how did the traditional path bring so many of us here?

FINANCIAL LITERACY: THE SOLUTION OR A COP-OUT?

A study showed 40 percent of Americans wouldn't be able to handle a four-hundred-dollar unexpected expense.[17] That's a scary number. Not only is the traditional way of life not producing positive results for millennials and Gen Z, but it looks like Gen X is suffering too.

Why are so many people struggling to manage money?

---

17 abcnews.go.com/US/10-americans-struggle-cover-400-emergency-expense-federal/story?id=63253846

Is it stagnant wages? Maybe.

Is it the cost of living? Potentially.

Is it the fact that many of us haven't had access to financial literacy education? As a starting point, I'm going to say this is a resounding *yes*.

When I say financial literacy education, I don't mean writing a check or balancing a budget. I'm talking about fiduciaries, predatory loan practices, compound interest, and how learning about money can quite literally make or break us. The fact that investing is the key to long-term financial success—not saving. The difference between mutual funds and ETFs. Why making more money doesn't matter, if you don't know how to manage it. How you can be broke making $100,000 and rich making $40,000. That a four-year degree isn't the only route to success. That student loans can cripple you, and credit cards can ruin your life, or be incredible tools to reduce risk and make cash back.

When I call lack of access to financial literacy education one of the major contributing factors to the crises in North America, I typically get a lot of pushback. Responses vary from, "You can't budget your way out of living paycheck-to-paycheck" to "Telling me *not to spend my money* won't change my situation." I get it. Poverty is a real thing. But there is a big difference between being broke and living in poverty. Living in poverty is when some external, extenuating circumstance impacts your ability to thrive economically. Poverty is not a choice.

Being broke, on the other hand, is when you're struggling with money based on your choices. It's actually a beautiful place to be, because if your situation is based on what you've done, then you can be the one to get yourself out of it. Most believe there is nothing they can do about where they're at with their money, but in most cases, that couldn't be further from the truth.

Many people understand the phrase "living paycheck-to-paycheck" to mean they don't have any "extra money," and there's "nothing left over" each month. In reality, this statement tells me nothing about your true financial situation. Even 40 percent of six-figure earners claim to live paycheck to paycheck.[18] It's not about how much you earn or your ability to survive financially, it's all about what you're doing with your money. As 78 percent of American workers from various backgrounds, industries, and locations say they live paycheck-to-paycheck, this phrase loses even more of its meaning.[19] Many use it as a catch-all phrase to indicate they're not doing well financially. Often, it's used to describe the struggle or feeling of not having enough, and is accompanied by the thought that there's absolutely nothing that can be done to change the situation. But, as showcased by the fact that 40 percent of six-figure earners still claim to live paycheck-to-paycheck, we can see it's not a "money in" problem, but more of a "what we do with the money once it's here" problem.

If we aren't taught about financial literacy in public school, and the only way we learn about money is from watching how our parents view and use money, and the rules we are taught by society to follow to "live a good life" don't provide us with a good life, then it's easy to see why so many people are struggling. So many important life concepts are not taught in school, and personal finance is at the top of my "Why the heck not?" list because *everyone* uses money.

So why don't we learn about financial literacy in school? My theory is that public school teaches us to be workers—to work for someone else and to make them rich. In school, there is an emphasis on following the status quo and learning so you can get a good job, while ignoring the fact that you can get a great job (without the university debt) in a trade, or

18 fool.com/the-ascent/personal-finance/articles/40-of-americans-making-100k-live-paycheck-to-paycheck-report/

19 forbes.com/sites/zackfriedman/2019/01/11/live-paycheck-to-paycheck-government-shutdown/?sh=44e5bfeb4f10

that entrepreneurship is another path. School caters to and creates the average person—and remember what I said about the average person? They're in debt, increasingly unhappy, and work a job they hate (but are usually stuck working it because they're stuck on the treadmill). Public school teaches us to get *on* the treadmill, go into massive debt, become consumers, and never get off because when you always *owe* money, when you've already spent tomorrow's dollar, you must always work.

If school isn't teaching us and our parents aren't setting us up for success because they don't know better, where does that leave us? Think of it this way: Kids who had parents with college degrees were more likely to attend college. If your grandparents went to college as well, you may even have a "family school" you're expected to attend. Research shows that 80 percent of those raised by two graduates said their parents encouraged them to attend a four-year school, compared to 29 percent of those raised in families without a degree. More than one-third of those raised in no-degree families said they were encouraged to take a job or enter the military instead of going to school.[20]

This is because our parents are more likely to guide us down the path they know or the path they believe is available to us based on their own life experiences. The same can be said for families who invest and are financially literate themselves.

If the only place you're learning about money is from watching your parents or caregivers use money (unless they're explicitly and intentionally teaching you), what usually happens is we get either a vicious cycle of poor money management passed down through generations, or parents who teach practical financial rules and information to their children starting at a young age. While the hand you're dealt makes a difference in how you start, it doesn't dictate how you finish.

---

20   theatlantic.com/education/archive/2014/04/are-college-degrees-inherited/360532

Imagine if you were taught about money (the right way) from a young age—if you learned that investing isn't scary, and that it is the only way to build real wealth and financial security. That you don't need to go into massive debt to get an education, and if you do, you should be working out your return on investment to make sure you're making a smart financial decision before you sign on the dotted line. That just because the bank approves you to spend a certain amount on a home, it doesn't mean you should. That money you save and invest in your twenties is worth twice as much as money you save and invest in your thirties due to compound interest. *Imagine where you could be if you were given the roadmap to success from the start.*

I have a friend whose son got some money for his fourteenth birthday. Can you guess what his son wanted to buy? Not an Apple Watch. Not an iPhone. He wanted to buy Apple stock. This kid was fourteen and already thinking about setting himself up for success in his future. While we have people in North America in their forties who still don't know what an index fund is, this kid was literally investing before he got his learner's permit.

Is this because the kid is inherently smarter? No.

It's because he was taught the importance of financial literacy from a young age.

I want you to think about how much money came into your life as a teenager and how much you spent on bullshit. I know I bought my fair share of crap (I'm looking at you, *J-14* magazine and sparkly hair ties). I'm dating myself here, but let's try out an example and see what a few minor changes in my childhood could have meant for my adult life:

Starting at twelve, I worked at a fast-food restaurant (yes, there were labor laws, but I lied on my application because if I wanted anything other than necessities as a kid, I knew I had to get it on my own). I started out making $5.95 an hour, working about twenty hours per week, which amounted to about $515 per month or $6,188 per year. I wouldn't have paid any taxes because my annual earnings were below the threshold. If you can't relate to getting a "real job" at that age, think about the money you earned (or could have earned) mowing lawns, washing your neighbor's car, or babysitting.

Now let's say I saved and invested even half of this, roughly $257 a month. Next, we'll assume a 10 percent annual return, which is the average return of the S&P 500 over the last hundred years. (We'll get more into the details of how to do this in a later chapter, but humor me here.) This would mean making 10 percent a year on my money, compounded. So at the age of twenty, I could have had $36,858.93. Look at that, almost the exact amount I took out in student loans to attend university (roughly $40,000).

Let's say I kept this up until I was twenty-five. I could have had over $79,000, and over $38,000 would have been *free* money I made by investing. That would have been enough for a down payment on a nice house. Now let's say I kept this up, investing the same amount every month until I was thirty. I could have had over $136,000. That $136,000 could have been enough to set me up financially for my entire life.

If you save and invest $100,000 by the time you're thirty-five, even if you never save another dollar, you will retire a millionaire. Anything you invest over and above that first six-figure account will just get you to financial freedom sooner, where you no longer have to work for money... because **retirement isn't an age—it's a number in the bank.**

If I had invested $136,000 and left it alone, at fifty I could have had over $1,170,000. That's enough to retire comfortably on $46,800 a year without the risk of running out of money. This is based on the 4 percent rule and the Trinity study. If I had waited until the traditional age of retirement at sixty-five, I could have had over $5 million. Remember, I could have hit this number without ever saving another dollar after the age of thirty, just by setting myself up for financial success from a young age.

My preteen income of $257 a month is only $8.57 a day. Meanwhile, you might be thinking, *Nicole, I don't have $257 a month.* Well, how much do you have? How can you save or make more? Can it be saved by forgoing Starbucks before work? Skipping fast food at lunchtime and packing a lunch instead? Cutting out subscription services, which the average consumer spends $273 on per month?[21]

Can it be made by picking up a part-time job? Delivering packages for Amazon? Driving Uber or Lyft? Grocery delivery? A side hustle?

Now this isn't to say you can't ever eat out or have your Starbies, because spending money is not the enemy—it's spending out of alignment with our true values and goals that becomes the problem. It's spending out of habit, without considering the opportunity or tradeoff costs, that keeps you stuck. If you work out the numbers (which we'll do later) and decide that you're happy with where your money is going when you include your daily expenses, then that's amazing. The key here is to ensure you know both what you are agreeing to and what you're forgoing to be happy with the outcome and impact it has on your life. You see, the key here is to ask "how can I" and start looking for opportunities in the face of adversity. If you say, "I can't," it will become a self-fulfilling prophecy.

How many kids get holiday money and birthday money and spend it on stuff that just clutters their house? They play with it for ten minutes before it gets added to the pile of other stuff they don't care about anymore. What if they were taught to use a portion of that to set themselves up for a real lifetime of success? With the powers of financial literacy, one person in a family—changing the narrative—could set their entire lineage up for a

---

21 zdnet.com/article/average-consumer-spending-273-per-month-on-subscription-services-report/

lifetime of success. If you had started building your net worth before you were even old enough to drive, how set could *you* be right now? Now, am I saying that every kid needs to invest? No. But the earlier we start learning about this stuff, the better we can plan for our futures.

My mom's favorite quote is, "If only I knew then what I know now"—and it's true. Hindsight is 20/20. How many times have you thought to yourself, *Ugh! I wish I could go back five or ten years and make different choices—* thinking about the things you could have done then to set you up for success today? Even though you can't, don't be too hard on yourself. You did the best you could with the information you had at the time.

Imagine if financial literacy education was accessible to everyone, not just private-school kids being primed to be the next big CEO. Imagine if people knew investing isn't *for* the rich, but *how* you become rich. Imagine if we taught our children the dangers of credit cards and overextending themselves financially, instead of using them to buy ourselves a treat, or when we don't have the cash for something. Maybe it wouldn't change everything for everyone right now today, but what could it do for future generations?

Just as college-educated parents are more likely to have kids who go to college, kids who come from families that are financially literate and *talk openly* about money are more likely to become financially successful themselves—whatever that means to them.

To some people, financial success means owning a lot of things: getting the G Wagon, a pair of Louboutins, and eating at all the most expensive restaurants.

But that's not how I define it.

My personal financial success doesn't look like a bunch of stuff, because I realized a long time ago that the only thing that's really finite in this world is my time. So I prioritize ways to own my time, so I can spend it however I please. Financial success looks to me like sleeping in on a Tuesday, having a bubble bath at three in the afternoon on a Thursday, breakfast with my husband, being able to show up at all of my kids' sporting events. I want the freedom to do what I want, when I want, and not have to report to anyone else.

To some, this could be as simple as not thinking about the cost of ordering guac when they go out to a restaurant. To others, this could mean having the ability to support their parents, maybe work part-time, maybe get a job they truly love and enjoy, instead of taking one they hate *just for the money.*

Winning with money is not that hard, once you know what to do. Did you know that 80 percent of millionaires are first-generation?[22] They didn't have families that set them up with the money they have now, and studies show they're not driving around in Range Rovers or wearing Gucci belts. They're people who know what they want and go after it, instead of falling for societal expectations, bullshit, and marketing ploys attempting to get you to spend more to keep up with the Kardashians.

HOW SOCIETY LEADS US ASTRAY

So who is this "society," and why are they so hellbent on leading us astray?

Merriam-Webster defines *society* as a community or group of people having common traditions, institutions, and interests.[23] Society is closely

---

22 washingtonpost.com/wp-srv/style/longterm/books/chap1/millionairenextdoor.htm
23 merriam-webster.com/dictionary/society

entwined with culture—one could not exist without the other.[24] Society dictates our culture, what is acceptable or not acceptable. It presents the unwritten rules a person follows as they move through life—even if no rules are actually spoken or posted. Whereas culture is essentially the unwritten rules of what we believe to be acceptable or common, or the "right" behaviors based on nuances we've accepted as fact, passed down to us as tradition by our families, friends, teachers, and communities.

An example that is spoken about a lot in sociology (the study of society and why we do things) is the culture of fast-food restaurants. Think about your favorite fast-food restaurant and the process you go through to eat there. You walk in, stand in line, order from the menu board behind the cashiers, pay for your food, take your tray to a table to sit down and eat, then throw your wrappers away when you're done, and leave. The rules are not posted and no one is there guiding you on what to do next; you just know what to do.

Imagine you did something different. Imagine you sat down at your table and shouted your order at the cashier, demanding to be served where you were seated. Imagine you brought your garbage to the cashier instead of to the trash bins provided, or instead of standing in line, you went into the back kitchen and made your own food. Even though these rules aren't posted anywhere, you *know* those actions wouldn't be received well—and you'd probably be asked (or forced) to leave.

We live in a traditional society, where what we do, what we believe is right, and what we pass down to future generations is what has been done in the past. How many times have you heard, "But we've *always* done it this way"? In sociology, traditional society refers to a society characterized by an orientation to the past, not the future, with a predominant role for

---

24   opentextbc.ca/introductiontosociology/chapter/chapter3-culture/

custom and habit,[25] which translates to, "This is how things have always been done, so this is the way we are going to continue to do them." Anyone who's ever worked with *that person* knows what I'm talking about. You know, the one who has worked there for years and has an extremely inefficient way of doing things, but is not open to feedback—*especially* if it means trying something new, and even if it makes more sense, saves time, saves money, etc. They are stuck in their ways and stuck in their tradition—yes, *that* person. That's who I imagine society to be in human form: Martha from Receiving, who takes hours to manually calculate all of the sales numbers for the night, when she could just export to an Excel sheet and be on her way in minutes (but she doesn't trust computers).

Great, so now we know who society is, and that there's an emphasis on tradition and culture which form the unwritten rules all of us are expected to live by, but how does this set us up for failure? Well, it sets us up for failure because the world we live in today isn't the world our parents or grandparents lived in.

- Approximately 90 percent of Americans born in the 1940s earned more than their parents by age thirty, and this number dropped to 50 percent among Americans born in the 1980s.[26]

- Millennials also have a lower net worth ($10,400 in 2013) than Gen X had ($18,200 in 1995).[27]

- Millennials have more student debt, though getting a college degree has become more necessary.

---

25 govtgirlsekbalpur.com/Study_Materials/Geography/GEOG_PART_II_HONS_Main_Features_ of_a_Traditional_Society.pdf

26 science.org/doi/pdf/10.1126/science.aal4617

27 nytimes.com/2015/08/02/opinion/sunday/were-making-life-too-hard-for-millennials.html

- Millennials are more likely to live with their parents than previous generations.

- Millennials are more tied to work because "logging in" from home is easier than ever, resulting in less work/life balance.

- Childcare is more expensive for millennials now than it was for their parents when they had kids.[28]

- We constantly have the highlight reel of someone's life in our face on social media, reminding us of the things we "don't have" and creating a sense of lack.

- We are getting pressure to "keep up with the Joneses" from people we know and from anyone with an online presence.

- We are being targeted with ads specific to who we are and our buying habits at all hours of the day, increasing the probability of us spending more and buying things we don't need, all in the name of "keeping up."

Compared to our grandparents, we are dealing with a completely different set of circumstances, and winning in those new circumstances is going to require a new set of traditions, new culture, and new rules. The society we live in today tells us to be a consumer—to treat yourself in the name of self-love no matter the cost, that you're being cheap if you want to save money, or you're depriving yourself of "living your best life," and that living in debt is normal. All of this is to keep you buying and on the treadmill. It's to keep you lining the pockets of companies that profit from making you feel like who you are and where you're at is not enough.

---

28   businessinsider.com/millennials-lives-compared-to-gen-x-baby-boomers-did-2018-3#millennials-
are-shelling-out-more-on-childcare-than-previous-generations-were-7

Advertising keeps you buying things you don't need to impress people you don't even like by making you feel less-than, so you'll part with your hard-earned dollars. **Advertising does a really good job at making you believe your wants are needs.**

How many times have you said, "OMG I need that new iPhone!" Do you actually *need* it, or do you just want it because marketers have made you believe your life won't be complete until you get the next and best? That you're no longer cool unless you have the newest model. That you're missing out if you don't make the purchase, even though the one you have serves you in every way you *need* it to. That once you buy their product, you will be *happier.*

It's quite the concept, isn't it? That buying things makes us happy. But that's exactly what good marketers make you believe, whether you realize it or not. While more things do make us happier, such happiness only extends to a certain point. With each new purchase and experience, we get more happiness and more fulfillment—like your first car, first trip, or first apartment—but unbeknownst to us, this happiness eventually plateaus. We keep buying more and more shit, hoping to reach that next level of happiness, but it never comes. Unfortunately, this doesn't stop us from forever trying to fill that void with more things, creating the perfect storm for advertisers to help them sell their next want as a need that will finally bring you the joy you've been seeking.

PREVAILING WISDOM (TRADITION) IN SOCIETY: START A BUDGET

Impulse-buying and spending beyond our means is one reason many of us are at odds with our finances. Even though society, culture, tradition, and "keeping up with the Joneses" are partly to blame for us feeling okay overspending (because *everyone does it*), society is also the first to tell us that our money problems are simply a math problem. You're only struggling financially, stuck in debt, or unsure of the best tactics to save and invest because you haven't written out your expenses on a piece of paper. Like a budget is the magic-pill solution, and once you start that spreadsheet, it will be easy to stick to. That what we really need to do is just restrict ourselves. Cut out everything fun and everything we love. That our coffees and avocado toast are the reason we're broke. Society tells you to budget, not because it's the best way to manage your money (studies prove otherwise), but because they have no other tools in their arsenal.

Research shows 74 percent of Americans say they keep a budget,[29] but if they work so well and are so easy to implement, why are so many people still struggling? Why do 79 percent fail to follow their budgets? It's simple. Budgets don't address the real issue. They are nothing more than an externally imposed solution to an internal problem. We all *know* we should be saving more, spending less, investing, paying down our debt, and not buying that random shit on Amazon, but we don't do it. A budget doesn't solve the muck beneath the surface of why we're not taking positive action with our money.

Believe it or not, most millionaires don't keep a budget.[30] It's because 1) budgeting (or couponing for that matter) will never make you rich, and 2) budgeting focuses on tactic, without understanding that good personal finance is 80 percent mindset and behavior and only 20 percent tactic. I don't use one, and it wasn't until I stopped using one and discovered a better way to manage my money that I started to see real change. You don't need a budget to be successful with money and in actuality, your budget could be the reason why you're broke.

29   cnbc.com/2019/12/26/consumers-overspend-by-7400-a-year-here-are-weekly-trouble-spots.html

30   businessinsider.com/millionaires-no-budgets-esi-money-millionaire-interviews-2018-12

CHAPTER 2

A **BUDGET** WON'T SOLVE YOUR **PROBLEMS**

Your budget could be the reason why you're broke. Let that sink in. It's a crazy concept, because it goes against the unwritten rules of society and what we've been taught unknowingly throughout our entire lives.

Money problems? Create a budget.

In debt? Create a budget.

Overspending? Create a budget.

It's been promoted as the magic-pill solution that automatically solves all your financial problems. More realistically, a budget is like the diet pill of the financial industry. Tell anyone you need help managing your money, and the immediate response will be, "Have you created a budget?" It's sold as this easy, one-size-fits-all solution. Just write out your expenses, and everything is solved.

Sorry, Brenda, we're not overspending, failing to pay down our debt, or impulse-buying because we are completely unaware (at least most of us aren't)—we're doing it for a variety of reasons a budget doesn't address. We're trying to fill emotional voids, to meet perceived needs based on what marketers tell us we must buy to be more cool, popular, and successful. We're buying because we're seeking happiness, joy, and fulfillment, because we feel stuck in other areas of our lives. We're struggling with our mental health, we're following what we've seen our parents do, we're catching FOMO, or maybe we just don't believe success is possible for us because we're stuck in a fixed mindset. A budget solves absolutely none of those things.

A budget gives you short-term results based on restriction and shame, and in the long run, it puts you into a vicious cycle of restriction and then bingeing because you feel deprived. Feelings of deprivation, and not working through the underlying causes of where you are with money and why, will lead you to binge-spend because you "deserve it." Then you'll go back to budgeting and feeling shame about the "hard work" you undid, and the cycle will start all over again.

Do you remember the show *The Biggest Loser*, where they brought people on who were able to lose unimaginable amounts of weight in a super short period of time? People would lose hundreds of pounds by working out multiple times a day and cutting calories to an unrealistic degree. These people would have mind-blowing results while they were on the show, but did you ever hear about their dirty little secret? After the show ended, 93 percent of the people the producers followed up with had regained all of the weight they'd lost.[31] Why? Well, because the show didn't address the underlying reasons why these people were overweight to begin with. There was no support to help them understand their *why*, and they didn't help them change their lifestyle. They just put them on a strict plan that was only feasible in the short term.

We all know diets get short-term results, and real improvement to your weight or health comes from a lifestyle change. If I only ate broccoli for the next three months, would I lose weight? Sure. Is it sustainable? Absolutely not. I can't eat only broccoli forever. Eventually, I'd end up craving other foods so

---

31 businessinsider.com/new-show-biggest-loser-winners-regained-weight-big-fat-truth-2017-6

badly that I would surely binge and overeat. The same thing happens when we budget. We do well for one, two, maybe three months...but then we fall off.

To illustrate my point, let's consider a scenario I've seen in one of my own students. The student, let's call her Sally, comes into our financial literacy program believing her problem is that she doesn't make enough money, as she's living paycheck-to-paycheck. Sally is going into debt, having trouble saving, and because of this, she is not hitting her financial and life goals.

Prevailing wisdom would tell Sally that the answer to her problems is a good budget—but she's tried budgeting many times before, without any long-term success. She would create a budget, do well the first month, okay on the second month, but generally by the third month would start having problems. Sometimes it would be unexpected expenses coming up that Sally hadn't accounted for, causing her to "steal" from other budgeted categories, leaving her lacking financially in certain areas. This lack created feelings of restriction and deprivation, so she'd start to spend more on things for herself as a way to compensate. Then she'd feel guilty about not sticking to her budget, and start believing that "this money thing is just too hard."

Belief that money was too hard, or that she just wasn't good with money, were thoughts that became ingrained in her, causing her to give up entirely—if what she believed was true, then any effort to change would be futile.

Did Sally fail at budgeting because she just didn't try hard enough? Or did the budget fail to understand the real reason Sally was living paycheck to paycheck?

You see, Sally actually grew up in the lower middle class. She never had new clothes, always wore hand-me-downs from her siblings, and can vividly recall being bullied for it in school. It was extremely traumatizing for Sally, and created a lot of problems for her emotional well-being and self-esteem that carry into her adult life today. So now that Sally has a big-girl job and her own money, she's subconsciously made it a point to always be dressed in the best. She wears designer and wouldn't be caught in anything "out of style." She puts on a show of being who she wants to be seen as through her purchases, and tries as hard as possible to buy things that distance her from who she believes she used to be.

Sally makes six figures a year and has every ability to live a financially stable life, but she spends without thinking about the tradeoff cost when it comes to clothing because she spent so long feeling deprived as a child, and is working so hard to be seen as the person she *wants* to be today.

The budget was a solution to a problem that no one took the time to uncover or truly understand. No matter how hard Sally budgets, no matter how "disciplined" or "motivated" she gets, without actually working through her beliefs about herself, what money is, and her true values (the psychological aspect of personal finance), money will never be effortless or easy for her.

It may seem innocuous at first, but taking the problem the student believes they have at face value is a huge mistake—because more often than not, people are looking at the symptom, and not the cause. The symptom is the presenting problem: living paycheck to paycheck, not being able to save, not paying off your debt, feeling like you're "falling behind" financially; the cause is *why* those things are happening.

It's a lot easier to treat the symptom than the cause, because discovering the *why* behind you being where you're at can take more effort and work—but that's where all the magic happens.

As our example with Sally showed, and you may have experienced, many people claim to live paycheck to paycheck—and although that term may indicate a lack of sufficient funds to pay for one's lifestyle, it doesn't provide the reason as to *why.*

SCARCITY MINDSET

A budget focuses on restriction and a mindset of lack and scarcity, which are never conducive to building wealth. What is a scarcity mindset, and how does it show up in the way we live and spend? A **scarcity mindset** believes there is not enough, and there will never be enough—and budgets reinforce ideas of scarcity and lack by making you write down and account for every dollar, "stealing" from different categories to make the numbers balance out. People with a scarcity mindset believe the world is like a giant pizza, and if anyone else takes a slice, there's less for them. When you have a scarcity mindset, no matter how big or small your dreams are, you believe you will never have enough to achieve them (even if your dream is just to be able to pay your bills), and this causes anxiety and worry every day. This worry and anxiety then prevent you from focusing on long-term financial goals because you're anxious and stuck in today.

Additionally, the worry and anxiety you experience from scarcity mindset prevents you from working toward your goals because, psychologically, you believe there's no point, you're stuck, there's no changing your situation, and you'll never have enough—so *why bother?* Even if you think you want to change, your actions will not align, and you will self-sabotage and get in your own way. Scarcity takes a lot of mental energy, constantly worrying about what you don't or can't have. It causes you to focus more on the bill that needs to be paid, the debt that's mounting, or the stress of the present, and stops you from being able to plan for your future. When your brain is operating in scarcity, it's like a computer running ten programs at once. It gets bogged down. It runs slower. When you're anxious and stressed, you are only capable of focusing on the "right here, right now." You don't have the mental bandwidth to think about anything else, and this lowered mental bandwidth leads to poor short-term decision-making.

A study by a Princeton psychologist and Harvard economist, Eldar Shafir, reports, "On average, a person preoccupied with money problems exhibited a drop in cognitive function similar to a thirteen-point dip in IQ, or the loss of an entire night's sleep."[32] When you operate from a scarcity mindset—the kind of mindset that a budget reinforces—you're not operating at peak performance, you're making bad decisions, you're not paying debt (or you're overpaying debt to the point of missing other financial obligations), you're overspending, and you're not working toward your long-term goals. Since budgets set you up for failure by ultimately leading to an inevitable inability to stick to your restrictive budget diet, that failure further reinforces the negative beliefs you have about yourself and your ability to get ahead financially. Internally, those beliefs resonate like a looming cloud of negativity in your mind: *Of course this didn't work. Nothing ever works. I always fail with money when I try to get ahead. I'll always live in this paycheck-to-paycheck cycle. Everyone struggles with money, so I'll always struggle with money.* These thoughts reinforce the negative fixed mindset. Mindset plays a huge role in your ability to achieve success in your life. If you believe something is not possible for you—that where you are right now is where you'll always be—then you won't seek the knowledge or put forth the effort to change. You'll stay stuck. What you believe becomes a self-fulfilling prophecy.

And I've seen it firsthand with our students: an inability to make good financial decisions because of the pervasive fear that they don't have enough, and will never have enough.

Let's take Jane, for example. When Jane came into our program, she had a scarcity mindset. Because of this system of beliefs, she was an avid saver—always thinking she would never have enough money, so she made it a priority to keep every penny she could get her hands on. Although she had five-figure savings, she also had five-figure credit card debt that she had been trying to pay for months with no success—the number on the bill just kept growing. To an outsider, the answer may seem pretty simple—use a

---

32 princeton.edu/news/2013/08/29/poor-concentration-poverty-reduces-brainpower-needed-navigating-other-areas-life

portion of the savings to start paying down the credit card debt (since it was at an astounding 24.99 percent interest)—but to Jane, it wasn't so simple. The savings made her feel safe and secure; even though she had enough to pay off her card in full and still have a sizeable emergency fund, she felt uncomfortable at the thought of using any of her savings to pay down the debt that just kept growing.

Other examples of how a scarcity mindset may show up in your life:

- You feel guilty for spending any amount of money, even if it's on things you planned and saved for

- You feel bad using, or won't let yourself use, your emergency fund *for emergencies* (this is something I see a lot of—the thought that, by using your emergency fund, you've now "fallen behind," when in fact that's exactly what you had those funds for)

- You play it small and don't believe you can have more in life—this can manifest itself by way of setting smaller goals than you'll truly be happy with

- You see other people achieving things that you want to achieve as an indication that now there isn't enough for you (for example, if a colleague gets a promotion, you take it as a sign that now there wouldn't be one for you)

- You don't believe you deserve more money, or can make or have more money

Wondering if you have a scarcity mindset when it comes to money? Ask yourself these questions to help determine if you're operating with scarcity-based beliefs:

1. Do you constantly worry about money? Is money always on your mind (in a negative way)?

2. Do you believe your current financial situation will be where you are forever, and there's no real way to change it?

3. Do you believe that money will always fly out of your life?

4. Do you believe that people who have money are "lucky," and that their success was only "by chance"?

5. Do you believe that spending money is bad?

6. Do you avoid taking any risks with your money, no matter how calculated (i.e., the thought of investing scares the living crap out of you)?

7. Do you believe money is for saving, not for spending, and thus feel an immense amount of guilt or shame when you spend?

If you answered yes to any of these questions, it's possible that you have beliefs aligned with a scarcity mindset.

GROWTH MINDSET VS. FIXED MINDSET

Carol Dweck's book *Mindset* was my first introduction to the concept that mindset plays an important role in our success. Psychologist Carol S. Dweck, PhD, has spent years researching how people think; how they process information, thoughts, and the things that happen to them; and how this impacts their ability to overcome adversity, challenges, and obstacles in their lives to find success. In her book, she clearly outlines the difference between a growth mindset and a fixed mindset, and through her studies, she has found that people who exhibit the qualities of a growth mindset typically end up leading more successful lives. Why? Their **growth mindset** sees challenges as opportunities to learn, grow, and figure out how they can get the result they want. Those with a growth mindset know we may not all become Albert Einstein, but with the right energy, knowledge, timeline, and grit, we can all accomplish success according to our individual definitions of it. Those with a **fixed mindset**, on the other hand, believe we are who we are—our level of intelligence, personality, and/or current situation are fixed, and there's no changing them. While a growth mindset thinks, "Rome wasn't built in a day," a fixed mindset thinks, "If Rome wasn't built in a day, then it wasn't meant to be." To an individual with a fixed mindset, every challenge in the pursuit of a goal is a message that *it isn't achievable for them*.

Let's consider two examples that demonstrate the difference between someone with a growth mindset and someone with a fixed mindset, how that could show up in day-to-day interactions, and the results of those beliefs in their lives. Imagine there are two people, and the exact same events happen to them over the course of a day: 1) they are late to work, 2) they overdraw their bank account buying lunch because they forgot to bring a lunch from home, and 3) they get reprimanded by their boss for doing a poor job on a report they put together.

FIXED MINDSET

Sally is late to work, which upsets her. She's been late every day for the past week. She's been missing her alarm because she keeps forgetting to plug in her phone overnight, and it dies before morning. She believes this is just further evidence that she is an irresponsible person who never does anything right, and figures she'll just end up continuing to be late. She internalizes the idea that *she is just someone who is never on time*.

At lunchtime, Sally checks her bag and realizes she left her lunch on the counter at home. She's only got a couple dollars in her checking account and has a maxed-out credit card, but she needs to eat, so she goes into overdraft on her debit card and racks up another twenty-dollar fee in addition to the cost of her lunch. Even though she specifically made that lunch so she could save money, she's now lost the money for the overdraft and for her lunch purchase, and the food on the counter has gone to waste. She believes this is just more evidence that she's irresponsible and will never actually be able to save money because every time she tries, *something* happens.

After lunch, Sally gets called into her boss's office to discuss a report she put together the week before. He says it's not her best work, and tells her it needs to be redone. Sally sees this as reinforcement that she can never do anything right, that she'll probably get fired because her boss obviously hates her, and then she'll be in an even worse position financially.

Sally goes home that day feeling horrible, defeated, unable to do anything right, and as if she is doomed to always struggle with money because she's just not good at it.

GROWTH MINDSET

Fred is also late to work and has been late every day for the past week. He's also been missing his alarm because he is forgetting to plug in his phone overnight, and it's dying before morning. Fred decides that 1) this is obviously not working for him, so tonight, when he gets home, he's going to pull out his traditional alarm clock to make sure he doesn't miss his alarm in the future, and 2) he's going to put a Post-it note on his bedroom door to remind him to set his alarm clock before he goes to bed. He decides he'll give himself a week to see if these strategies secure his on-time arrival at work, and if not, he'll go back to the drawing board and figure out a better way to stay on time in the mornings.

At lunchtime, Fred checks his bag and realizes he left his lunch on the counter at home. He's only got a couple dollars in his checking account and has a maxed-out credit card, but he needs to eat, so he goes into overdraft on his debit card and racks up another twenty-dollar fee in addition to his lunch. Fred isn't happy about this mishap, but knows he likely forgot his lunch because he was so rushed in the morning from missing his alarm. He doesn't like the fact that he's had to spend the extra money, but he decides to pick up some overtime to make up for it and to help put him back on track.

After lunch, Fred gets called into his boss's office to discuss a report he put together the week before. He knew it wasn't his best work, because he'd rushed it because of being behind all week from missing his alarms and being late. He tells his boss he'll get it redone that evening, since he's planned to work overtime. He reassures his boss that he's already put measures in place to ensure it doesn't happen again.

Fred goes home that evening feeling good about his plan. He knows what he will do differently in the future to get a more desirable result, and if that plan doesn't work, he's brainstormed some other ideas he can try. He's working overtime to help rebuild his savings, and he knows his boss will be happy with the report he redid because he went above and beyond to show his commitment to improvement.

> Sally and Fred had the exact same day, but the way they each thought about it was different. The differences in their mindsets determined their individual beliefs about themselves, their beliefs about the things that happened throughout their day, what they interpreted those things to mean about themselves, as well as how they internalized their thoughts and beliefs and allowed them to shape their day, their attitude, and their success in reaching their goals.

When you budget and fail, you push yourself into a scarcity or fixed mindset, which inherently alters your ability to have success. Additionally, overreliance on a budget as the solution to your problems prevents you from seeking out the underlying cause—the reason *why* you're doing what you're doing—and figuring out the *why* is imperative to you being able to craft your individual roadmap to success.

Wondering if you may have a growth or fixed mindset? Ask yourself these questions to help determine which camp you may fall into:

- When something bad happens in your day, do you believe it's a reflection of who you are as a person (it is your fault)?

- If you try something and fail, do you believe this indicates the task is too hard for you, or not possible to accomplish?

- Do you believe that, to have success, people need to be naturally talented at the task?

- Do you feel attacked by criticism, even when it's meant to be constructive?

- Do you act impulsively, without considering your decision-making?

- Do you believe someone's intelligence, personality, or other traits are fixed and cannot be changed much?

- If a task becomes challenging, do you easily give up?

- Do you look for opportunities to take the easy route, to avoid putting yourself in a situation where you may fail?

Answering yes to some or all of these points could indicate an inclination toward a fixed mindset.

WHY IS THERE SUCH AN EMPHASIS ON BUDGETS IN OUR SOCIETY?

All of that said, it raises the question: If budgets don't work, why does society put such an emphasis on them? Furthermore, why are budgets the number one "financial tool" talked about in school, pushed on us by our families, and relied upon by so much of the world? And what is it about a budget that makes people think it just might work?

A budget feels like a long-term solution because it helps you feel like you're in control, like you are taking action toward fixing your financial situation. You're getting to the bottom of it. You believe you've done all you need to do. You've taken the magic pill. You've reduced your life, wants, needs, and troubles down into a spreadsheet of numbers, of dollars and cents. It can feel good to take the step because it feels like you're making progress. Because *something is better than nothing, isn't it?*

A budget is so enticing because it is literally the easiest thing we can do, when we look at all the options we have for potentially enacting change in our lives. A budget is the magic-pill solution you can put in place without having to do any of the real work. A budget allows you to think everything will change after spending fifteen minutes with a spreadsheet.

Our society puts an emphasis on quick fixes because we are drawn to easy choices. We'd rather take a pill than change our diet and start exercising. We'd rather have a glass of wine than learn stress management. We'd rather get a prescription than make a lifestyle change. We'd rather put a Band-Aid on a problem than look at the root cause, because that would be more work. We are eager for success, and we thrive on "getting it done." We want instant benefit, but this creates a false sense of security that prevents us from looking at the reasons why we are here in the first place, and is the reason we never actually do the work that is necessary to see real change. To break out of this, the first thing we need to do is acknowledge that a budget limits our control.

Our society and school systems thrive by making us believe everything will work out if we just follow a certain set of rules. School doesn't teach us to think. It teaches us to follow, to memorize, and to assimilate. It tells us that we should all fit into this perfect little box and that, by following a set of rules, our life will always be exactly what society wants it to be. But as many of us grow, we realize we don't fit into this box—and even if we could, we don't want to. We strive to be individuals, but society wants us to be carbon copies. A budget is a further extension of this. It tells you that your life, your expenses, your wants, your needs, your goals, and your desires can all be planned with a predetermined set of rules.

Two examples of budget-specific rules that I don't agree with are:

> **Rule 1:** Your housing should cost no more than 30 percent of your income.

> **Rule 2:** You should be saving 10 percent of your salary for retirement.

When you're following a set of formulas that was made without you in mind, there is no room in a budget to be individualistic. What if your housing is 50 percent of your income? Would the world burn down? What if you decided spending 50 percent of your income on housing *feels good to you*? Maybe you don't drive, you don't have kids, and you don't really spend much on going out, but you really enjoy living in the more expensive part of town. That lights your fire. That makes *you* happy. Yet a traditional budget says no. That's not allowed. You're straying from the box.

What happens when we focus on planning our lives based on who society tells us to be, not who we are or want to be? We falter. We feel like we're failing because we didn't take *ourselves* into consideration. Save 10 percent of your income for retirement? What's this based on? Have you worked out what your dream retirement looks like? Probably not. So we're out here saving 10 percent of our salaries for retirement, hoping, wishing, and praying that when we get there, we have what we need to live the life we want? What if, to live the life you want, you need more? What if you need less and could have spent more on life today? What if you learned that, if you found ways to increase your income or reduce your spending and save *more* than 10 percent, you could stop working well before the age of sixty-five? Remember, retirement isn't an age, but a number in the bank.

A budget also doesn't always account for life. Life is messy. Shit happens. There will always be unexpected expenses that arise. Medical bills. Death in the family. Unemployment. Getting into an accident. Your pet needing to go to the vet. Or something less innocuous, like your rent increases, your phone's screen breaks, or you get a parking ticket. When these unexpected expenses inevitably arise (because such is life), where does that leave us? A budget tells us to follow a set of rules, but it doesn't teach us how to think on the fly (or how to think critically at all). When something happens that doesn't abide by those rules, what do you do? Maybe you think it's easy to pivot, but the simple fact that 79 percent of Americans say they don't stick to their budget tells me otherwise, as referenced in our introduction. You don't need a budget. You need to learn what's important to you, and how to think critically about what you're spending and why. But society doesn't want us thinking, it wants us following. When you acknowledge that a budget limits the control you have in your life, you can begin to grow out of it and refocus your goals.

CHAPTER 3

IF NOT A **BUDGET,** THEN **WHAT**?

It's pretty clear at this point that we want to stay as far away from a fixed or scarcity mindset as possible, because what we believe about our lives and money becomes all the results we will have with money. And, if a budget is reinforcing beliefs of scarcity, lack, and fixed mindset, we probably want to steer clear of it.

But budgeting is the prevailing wisdom, the societal expectation, the unwritten (and written) rule of managing your money, passed down from generation to generation.

According to almost everyone, budgeting is the only way to manage your finances. So if we aren't going to budget, then how on earth are we supposed to control our spending and work toward our goals?

This was the dilemma I faced as I was working to change my financial situation. I budgeted hard while I was in university because it was the only type of "money management" I had ever been taught. I'd constantly been exposed to the Dave Ramseys, the Suze Ormans, and the Gail Vaz Oxlades of the world. The notions that spending money was bad, that being in debt was your own fault, and that struggling with money meant you were just a *money moron* were all things I'd learned from them. These financial gurus used shame, blame, and guilt to "help people manage their finances," so for a long time, I believed this was just the way it had to be.

As such, while I was in university I budgeted my money, and I budgeted hard. At that time, my favorite way to restrict my spending was the jar method. Have you heard of it? Essentially, what you do is take out the money you're *allowing* yourself in cash (note the scarcity/lack language here) and put it into glass jars. Each jar is labeled with your expense category: food, travel, clothes, entertainment, etc. Every budget cycle, I would go to the bank, take out the cash I was allowing myself for that week, and divvy it up between the jars. Sounds simple, right? Then you only spend what's in the jar, and this is supposed to bring awareness to your spending and keep you on track. Seems innocent enough. The intention behind the thought process is that you'll physically see (through the glass jars) when your money is running out in a certain category; it becomes an in-your-face call to change your spending habits, *like immediately.* If you don't buckle down for the rest of the week, you're likely to need to take money from another jar, and you'll have to physically watch yourself have less and less available for other things.

I never felt more anxiety than I did watching that money disappear each week. Every dollar I spent left me feeling an immense amount of guilt and stress because I was quite literally watching myself go broke. The thought of having to "steal" from another category crushed me and reinforced the notion that I was a failure of personal finance. Budgeting and the jar method made me feel that spending money was the enemy, that I couldn't be trusted to spend money responsibly (as shown by the fact that I had to keep taking from my other jars and watching the amounts dwindle), and that I just shouldn't spend at all. When you don't spend any money, you don't have any fun, so you never enjoy yourself, and you start to feel restricted. Just as severely restricting calories on a diet typically leads to binge eating, overly restricting spending typically leads to binge spending.

So I did as one does: I would restrict, and then when I couldn't take the restriction any longer, I would spend. It became a vicious cycle. I would do well with my jars for a month or two, but then I'd start to feel like I was really missing out on life. I would always justify things to myself: *Well, I've been working really hard in school. I've been sticking to my jars. I DESERVE to go out. I deserve to buy a new outfit. I deserve to spend, spend, spend until I find the silver lining to all this restriction.* This would lead me to spending until I found a little sliver of happiness, after being so stressed and anxious about money for so long.

I brought this mentality with me through graduation, but by the time I got to the corporate world in my first big-girl job, I felt like I had been restricted by living that #BrokeStudentLife for so long that I really *deserved* to spend. I was making more money than ever before. After all, I'd graduated university and worked my ass off to get here. Now that I had a coveted corporate job, I would be crazy *not* to spend that money on things that proved my success to others (I'm looking at you, $1,600 Mackage jacket). And the cycle continued: I spent money to meet an emotional need and a perceived societal notion that I was only successful if I *looked* successful. I searched for happiness in a purchase, and then I'd crash. After seeing what I spent, I'd restrict myself again. I was living in an almost constant state of buyer's remorse, but I couldn't stop shopping.

I worked so hard to get to where I was, and for a short while, I felt I had finally made it. It wasn't long before I started to believe I was falling behind—falling behind in life, falling behind on my goals, and falling behind financially. My social media was chock-full of people I knew buying houses, getting married, and having kids—all things I desperately wanted, but I was living paycheck to paycheck, in an endless cycle of spend/guilt/restrict/spend/guilt/restrict. I had no idea how I was going to pay back my $40,000 in student loans, let alone buy a freaking house in one of the most unaffordable housing markets in the world.

I could not figure out how people were doing it, and for a while, I continued to struggle. I believed this was my fate, and people like me just weren't lucky enough to reach those other financial goals. I started telling myself the only reason those people had what I wanted, and I didn't, was because they had help, they had handouts, they started from square five while I had to start from scratch. And I could have stayed here, in this victim mentality, and continued to let it to break me. Instead, I decided to get gritty. I decided to figure it out. I decided I wouldn't let this be my story. I knew there had to be another way. People were doing it, so it was possible. I just hadn't figured out the solution for my personal situation yet. If not budgeting, then what?

I decided to use my college degree and do a root cause analysis. This meant asking myself some basic questions that required me to be honest with myself. *Why am I truly here in this position? Why do I continue to overspend, even though overspending is preventing me from getting what I really want in life: marriage, a house, and kids?*

I'm sure a lot of you can relate to this. Every day, I thought about wanting to buy a house but not having enough saved up for one. I thought about wanting to get married, but having no idea how people could afford something like that. I dreamed about the day I'd feel like I could financially take care of myself, let alone take care of kids. Those were the real things I wanted in my life. Those were the things that would make me truly happy, but every day I was spending frivolously on crap, searching for happiness, while actively bringing myself further away from happiness. Admitting the truth to myself was a difficult but necessary first step in turning my situation around. Ultimately, the realization that my choices were preventing me from reaching my goals was a hard pill to swallow. I went to bed thinking about my goals and woke up wishing for them. I realized spending money I didn't have to buy shit I didn't need was sabotaging my ability to life my dream life. So I asked why, and why, and why again. I asked why over and over and over until I got to the root cause of everything—all the pain, all the mismanaged funds, all the problems I was having. After uncovering all the layers, what I found shaped the methodology that helped me pay off $40,000 of debt in eighteen months and build a $500,000 net worth in my twenties.

My root cause analysis revealed that I was overspending because I was searching for happiness, and I believed that happiness came from something external, something I bought, even though any happiness I got from purchases was always short-lived. So if happiness was the key, and happiness was what I was searching for, why was I following traditional rules and societal frameworks that quite literally were making people unhappy? Remember: The average person is in debt, unhappy, and working a job they hate (and the number of unhappy people is rising annually). Being restricted makes people unhappy. Bingeing feels good in the moment, but ultimately makes people unhappy. Upon these realizations, the frameworks I once believed in wholeheartedly began to unravel. I began to see how the traditional path we are sold is a lie and is the reason so many people are unhappy and struggling.

I realized that if I wanted something different, I had to do something different. If I didn't want what the average person had (unhappiness), then I had to do something extraordinary. I don't mean extraordinary in the sense that it had to be some crazy, out-of-this-world, hard-to-do phenomenon. Simply going against the grain and creating your own path *is* extraordinary because most people won't do it. I started to realize most people follow the traditional path and end up unhappy, hoping, wishing, praying for a change, without ever actually taking the action they need to make the change. It's unbelievable because, when I took a step back and really looked at my life, I began to see all the ways following this traditional path had set me up for failure.

Societal rules about life are all just contradictions leading us astray. They want us to save more and plan for the future, but we're also not supposed to waste an opportunity to enjoy life: #YOLO. We're supposed to go to school and get an education to propel our futures, but then we graduate with student loans that hold us back. We're supposed to keep up with the latest fashions, phones, and gadgets, but we're shamed for not being closer to financial goals like buying our first home. Saving money means you're good with money, but not spending money means you're stingy. Having the nicest car, clothes, and things shows people how successful you are, and it's okay to buy on credit because you deserve it—but don't ever speak about your debt, because debt is shameful. Working your way up the corporate ladder as a woman is commendable, but spending too much time working means you're a success-obsessed workaholic. It's understandable that our generation is crippled with anxiety, depression, and debt—these are the contradictory messages we are given about how we're "supposed to" live our lives.

I decided I was done with the BS. I was done listening to traditional advice and society and the unwritten rules. I realized that, to have real success, I needed to do the opposite of what I was told. Though we're told to restrict ourselves, to budget, and to feel shame and blame, what if I spent freely, without restriction, without shame, blame, or anxiety, and focused solely on happiness? True happiness. *But what was true happiness? Had I ever known it amidst all the perceived and fleeting happiness that came with spending money on things I wanted, or thought I needed to make me happy?* I realized I needed to find out what true happiness was to me. I needed to change the way I thought about money and how I viewed and used money.

I wanted to:

- Understand more about why I did the things I did, and how I could empower myself to do the things that were necessary to bring me closer to my goals.

- Know where my thoughts about money came from, how those thoughts shaped my life, and how I could rewrite them.

- Create a simple way to manage my money that didn't involve shame, blame, restriction, or anxiety.

- Create new money rules to run my life that would provide the opposite effect of budgeting (a.k.a. a feeling of freedom and happiness).

I needed to find ways to get more money without necessarily having to work more for it or change my lifestyle. I had to understand what purchases were personally worth the cost to me, which were not, and why. Learning all this started with me first learning that personal finance cannot be a one-size-fits-all approach because personal finance is personal.

Then, I needed to learn how to seek happiness in what I bought—true happiness—and to stop buying crap I didn't even really want or need to fill voids. Not only did I need to wake up and learn that I am in control of my life, but I needed to take control of my life. I could continue hoping, wishing, and praying for a change, *or* I could *choose* to be ready to go after my goals, to stop operating from a place of scarcity, lack, and a fixed mindset, to start looking at challenges as opportunities for growth, to get gritty, and start asking, "How can I?" instead of saying, "I can't," when faced with adversity. I wanted to learn the things that were truly going to make a difference in my financial health, instead of focusing on broke questions and sentiments. I needed to gain the understanding that I basically had to take everything society had taught me about money and life and turn it on its head. I had to rewrite the rules and make them work for me, instead of trying to contort myself to fit some predetermined plan that just didn't work. I was going to learn the real traps that prevent people from building wealth and how to prevent myself from falling into them, and to understand how my relationships (romantic or otherwise) impacted my ability to have success. Finally, I was ready to truly learn about saving, investing, and growing my money without sacrificing happiness to get there.

I've done the work, and now I'm here to share it all with you in the next seven chapters.

Are you freaking ready? Let's go!

CHAPTER 4

MONEY **MINDSET**

Ah, money mindset. I could write an entire book on this topic alone. That's how important (and eye-opening) this is. Although many don't realize it, our belief systems and the internal scripts and rules we've created about life all reflect the results we get in our lives, and changing where we're at, in any aspect, requires an internal audit of ourselves to see how we've gotten there.

This chapter is going to be the key to building your foundation to making money management easy. Remember: Personal finance is 80 percent mindset and behavior and only 20 percent tactic. While I'm going to teach you the tactics to grow your money while you sleep (yes, it really is possible to grow your money while you sleep, and not in some weird, scammy, MLM sort of way)—before I get into any of that, I first need to help you set the foundation all the other lessons will hinge upon.

What is **money mindset**? Money mindset is the set of beliefs and rules you hold about all things money-related, like earning, saving, spending, and debt. These are the rules and scripts you use to run your life, whether you realize it or not. They're internal, they're unconscious, and they determine the direction you go in without you even thinking about it because they're ingrained in your belief system. They're your default setting. Our mindset around money and the rules we developed to handle all our decision-making around money controls all the results we have in our lives with money. So mastering your money mindset is step one in becoming good with money, and it is imperative to your long-term success.

Money mindset is something a budget fails to address, and unfortunately, a lot of people fail with personal finance because they skip the beginning steps, not because it's difficult. They want the quick fixes, and they want the sexy stuff because what's sexier than waking up and seeing your bank account has grown without any effort on your part? As a financial coach, I see it all the time. No one wants the mindset stuff.

"Oh, I don't need that. I just need to learn how to invest. I need to grow my money. I need to make more of it."

What people don't understand is that amassing more of something doesn't automatically make you good with it. If we struggle to manage $1,000, we will struggle to manage $10,000 (until we learn how to do something different). Getting more money is a side effect of being good with money, not the other way around. You don't get good at it just because you have more. This is why so many lottery winners, pro athletes, and rappers go broke. In most cases, they had a lot of money, but they never took the time to set the foundation for the mindset of managing it. In many cases, these individuals went from living a lower– or middle-class life to amassing a large amount of wealth in a very short period of time. There are a variety of mindsets and beliefs that can come along with this, depending on what they were previously taught, or had seen, in relation to money through their earlier life experiences.

One potential mindset and belief system that could cause these athletes, lottery winners, and pro athletes to go broke is a kind of imposter syndrome: internally they still identify as someone who doesn't have money, or isn't good with money, so they unknowingly self-sabotage by spending everything they have to bring them back to what feels comfortable. I call this your money gauge.

Your money gauge is simply the amount of money that feels normal and natural to you, and can be formed through your earliest experiences with money. Did your family struggle with money? Was debt normal and expected? Or did your family have an abundance of money, where you never had to want for anything? These experiences shaped what you feel is normal when it comes to personal finance, and helped form your internal money gauge. If you don't work on your beliefs and mindset when it comes to money, you may unknowingly work to bring yourself back to "comfort"—even if this comfort is making you unhappy or preventing you from really achieving your goals.

Ever heard the saying, "Don't try to build your house without first pouring your foundation"? Personal finance, and learning any concept really, all starts with foundational knowledge that you will use to build upon. Foundational knowledge ensures the rest of what you learn makes sense. It's knowledge that is necessary for you to be successful with the future knowledge you learn. Failing to build your foundation of knowledge in personal finance with your mindset and behavior is like constructing a house on undeveloped land.

Imagine you get a plot of land and you're going to build your dream house. You're so excited! You can't wait to start designing your dream kitchen, choosing colors and décor—so much so that, when you find out it could take *months* to get the land ready to build on, you decide to skip that part. Who wants to spend time flattening the hills in the land, cutting down trees, installing cables and wires and plumbing for the utilities? That stuff is boring, it's not fun, it's probably expensive, and it just feels like more work than you want to do. You don't *want* to wait months to start putting your dream kitchen together. You want to do it now. You can already smell the incredible meals you're going to cook, as you envision yourself having people over for your housewarming party, sitting at your new bar, sipping cocktails, and eating hors d'oeuvres.

What's not a part of that picture? A construction worker grading your lot. So you skip it. You build your house on the land the way it is—lumps, hills, and all. Instead of cutting down the trees, you just build around them. Faster is better, and we want to get to living that dream we envisioned.

Then, when you go in to view the finished product, you're a little concerned. Your dream house is contorted, the floors are all slanted, and being inside makes you feel dizzy and a little sick. The beautiful marble you picked out for the floors is cracking because nothing is leveled. The floor plan makes no sense because there are cutouts around the preexisting trees. The lights don't turn on, it's freezing cold, and you have no running water. While, technically, you focused on the sexy stuff, it is the unsexy stuff that allows the sexy stuff to work and flourish.

You may believe your money mindset is great and there's nothing to learn or work on, but, in my experience, the people who say they have it all together are usually the ones who need the mindset work the most. The more you know, the more you realize how much you don't know.

There's this thing called the ego. It's that little voice inside your head that tries to tell you how life works. The ego's job is to keep you safe, and safety to the ego is the familiar, a.k.a. what it already knows. So the ego will do everything in its power to keep you stuck where you are because there, it knows what to expect. Even if where you are is bringing you unhappiness, even if it's not conducive to reaching your goals, and even if it's bad for you—it doesn't matter. The ego wants you there. The ego's rationale is usually: It's shit where I am. I know that, but I feel safe because at least I know *this* shit. I know what to expect. If I go out and venture into something new or try something different, it could be worse, because I don't know what to expect since I've never done it before. I don't know *that* shit. Since I know *this* shit, I choose to stay here.

This can be the reason people stay in bad relationships or bad jobs longer than they should. The fear of change overwhelms you (knowingly or unknowingly), and your ego causes you to rationalize the situation by putting an overwhelming emphasis on the "good" in where you are:

- "Oh well, sometimes they make me laugh."

- "Last year, my boss did say 'Happy Birthday' to me. That was nice."

- "I did get to work from home that one day last month."

From a financial standpoint, you may say to yourself:

- "Jenna has more debt than I do, so my situation must not be that bad."

- "I have food on the table and a roof over my head. There are others who are in worse positions."

- "Sometimes I have a hundred dollars left in my bank account at the end of the month, so I'm doing fine."

- "I'm okay where I am. It could always be worse."

As if "okay," "fine," and "it could be worse" are the yardsticks we want to use to measure success in our lives. Personally, mediocrity is not the yardstick I want to use to measure success in my life, and I don't think I know anyone who would be excited about looking back on their life in old age and thinking, "It was okay." Even just admitting there is something that needs to change can be difficult, because this can break down our sense of self and put our ego into overdrive. The ego doesn't want you to know it doesn't have it all figured out. It wants to place the blame on someone (or something) other than yourself.

Likewise, it's easy for us to fall into the pattern of thinking the only solution to our problems is to get more money because our ego wants us to believe where we are is fine, what we're doing is great, our situation is not our fault, and that everything would be different if we just *had more*. Our ego wants to blame our money problems on someone or something other than ourselves and our behaviors. Admitting there is something inside of us that may need to change is not usually a first option. For many, if they do admit something needs to change, it's only after catastrophe has struck.

The problem with all of this is that, for you to see change in your life, you first need to admit that something needs to change.

There are three steps to changing your life:

1. Admitting there's a problem, or there's something that needs to change

2. Seeking the knowledge necessary to solve that problem or enact the change in a meaningful way

3. Implementing what you've learned in your life

Most people won't even make it to Step 1, and that's why they'll stay stuck. They let their ego run their thoughts. Your thoughts become your beliefs, your beliefs become your actions, and your actions become the results you have in life. It all starts with our beliefs and mindset.

Many don't believe true change is possible, and they end up right. Ultimately, believing change is not possible becomes a self-fulfilling prophecy, because the brain believes what you tell it. If you tell your brain there is no way out, there will be no way out. Thinking change is impossible will cause you to continue looking for excuses as to why "it will never work," instead of solutions centered around what it will take to work. It's easy to fall into the trap of believing where you are right now is where you'll be forever, that the cards are just stacked against you, and there's no way out. I've been there, *I get it.*

For a long time, I believed I was the victim in my life, and I was angry about it. I was mad at my parents for not setting me up for success in the ways I believed they should have and for not providing me with a handout to start my life like I saw so many others get. I was mad at the government for letting student loan practices to become so predatory that I was allowed to take on $40,000 of debt for a degree when the bank would have never given me—an unemployed kid who really didn't know what she was getting herself into—a loan for anything else. I was mad the job market was so shitty—like, why did entry-level jobs require two years of experience? Why did wages not keep up with housing costs? Why? Why? Why?

Angry and full of questions, I could have stayed there, playing the victim, believing things were happening *to* me, that everything was out of my control, and that the system was rigged against me, so I could never win. I was stuck in a cycle of scarcity and fixed mindset, and had a negative belief system when it came to money. I saw money as a finite resource, one that I didn't have enough of, and one that I couldn't get more of.

But I just couldn't accept the idea that this had to be my fate. So I decided to take radical responsibility for everything in my life, even the stuff that wasn't my fault. I had to change my beliefs about what was possible for me, and what I had the ability to control. I took responsibility for my actions, my reactions, my efforts, my thoughts, my plans, my education—*my life.* When I did that, everything started to change. Everyone thought I started to get lucky, but that luck was nothing more than the result of me beginning to take radical responsibility for my actions and the results I had in life.

I distinctly remember a time when I felt like all I could do was win, which was a *big* change from the way I used to view my life (as a series of unfortunate events). The harder and smarter I worked, the more I took responsibility and action, the grittier I got, the more I looked adversity in the face and said, "How can I?" the more things continued to change. And the "luckier" I started to get.

There was a time when my vocabulary consisted of:

- I can't afford that.

- That's too hard.

- I'll never be able to do that.

- I'm not smart enough, good enough, or stable enough.

- Insert your favorite BS excuse here: _____.

I replaced the thought that I couldn't with the curiosity to find out how I could. If someone—anyone—has done what you want to do before, that means it *is* possible. You just haven't figured out the way. As you move forward in your personal finance journey (or in life, really), instead of saying, "I can't afford that," or, "I can't do that," ask: "How can I afford that?" and "How can I do that?" The shift to using these three magic words—*How can I?*—changed my life.

I started to believe that, even though I was starting from a different point than others, I still had the ability to achieve success. I could still build my dream life. It might take more time, I might have access to different resources, but I could figure out a way. If it's been done before, that means it *is* possible; I just hadn't crafted my own personal roadmap to success...yet.

I moved from a place of scarcity and lack to one of abundance and growth. I knew that, with the right passion, energy, knowledge, timeline, and grit, I could find my success. I knew that, by taking radical responsibility for every result I had in my life, I would be able to change it for the better. Maybe not today, maybe not tomorrow, but eventually I would get where I wanted to go.

Now, I can already hear the naysayers: "Nicole, taking responsibility for everything sounds toxic," and if that's what you're getting out of this section, you're thinking of it all wrong. Taking responsibility is not the same as taking the blame. There are tons of things that happened to me that sucked, that are totally and completely not my fault—and if you're a cycle-breaker, you know what I'm talking about. Growing up, my home life was tumultuous at best, which is why I dropped out of high school at the age of sixteen to move out and work full-time to support myself. While I don't blame myself for what happened to me in my childhood, I do take responsibility for how I went on living life after they happened—for the actions I took (or didn't take) and how that impacted my life. I'm also now taking responsibility to break the cycle, so my children don't have to heal from my unhealed traumas.

Let's look at an example.

Say you're out for a walk, and you cross on a green light. At the crosswalk, you even press the little button to make sure you get the walk signal, but as you're moving across the road, you get hit by a car. Is it your fault? No, you've done everything right. You took precautions, you followed the rules, and you obeyed the laws. You did what you were *supposed to do.* Something happened that was out of your control.

Now let's say the car accident breaks your leg, and you need surgery. After surgery, you need physical therapy to help you regain control of your muscles. You'll need to do special exercises to manage the rehabilitation and pain. Instead, you decide: *This wasn't MY fault. I did what I was supposed to do. I shouldn't have been hurt. It's the driver's fault for not stopping. It's the city's fault for not enforcing the rules of the road in this area. It's the car manufacturer's fault for not installing further safety measures to make sure pedestrians don't get hurt.* You're so mad about all of this that you decide not to spend the time and money necessary to rehabilitate your leg. You decide not to go to physical therapy, and you refuse to do the exercises. As a result, your leg doesn't get better. You have trouble walking. You're in pain. You may need a cane, or some other medical device to help you get around.

In this situation, you have a choice to make: You can spend the rest of your life struggling and in pain because what happened wasn't your fault, or you can take responsibility for the way you handle the shit life has thrown at you (because throwing shit is one of life's favorite pastimes). When you take responsibility, you do what needs to be done to change your situation. Life is always going to be hard, but the beautiful thing about life is that we get to choose our hard. Staying stuck is hard, making the change is hard. Ask yourself: which will you choose?

> Marriage is hard. Divorce is hard. Choose your hard.
>
> Obesity is hard. Being fit is hard. Choose your hard.
>
> Being in debt is hard. Being financially disciplined is hard. Choose your hard.
>
> Communication is hard. Not communicating is hard. Choose your hard.
>
> Life will never be easy. It will always be hard. But we can choose our hard. Pick wisely.
>
> —Devon Brough

This quote helps us to understand that everything in life is a choice. Although the way we grow up and experience money through those around us helps shape our initial money mindset, it's never too late to choose to reshape it in a way that may serve us better, based on our goals later in life. By saying you *can't* do something, you are giving *all* your power away. Could it be difficult? Sure. But when you prime your brain to look for possibilities and opportunities, you empower yourself to know that change is possible.

Consider those of us who grew up watching our parents struggle with money, living paycheck to paycheck, not making ends meet. Or those who saw consumer debt as a normal and natural thing. Or those who were never allowed to spend a dollar of their birthday money because "money is for saving, not spending." Or those who overheard conversations about how "rich people are assholes," and internalized the belief that having money makes you a bad person... Just because you've lived something, or your parents have lived something, or your grandparents have, that doesn't mean you need to continue living it. When we grow up under certain circumstances, what we see and hear can influence us to believe this is how life has to be. These become the unconscious money rules that run our life and determine our fate, whether we realize it or not.

Oftentimes, our money rules or beliefs are not in alignment with who we want to be. They are aligned with our current state of being, where we're at personally, professionally, and financially, but they're not conducive to the growth we need to get to our goals and dream life. They can become the rules we fall back on when making decisions that bring us further from our goals. These rules will guide us throughout life and either propel us forward or hold us back.

Imagine two different people—let's use Sally and Fred again in our example. We're going to look at different possibilities for sets of beliefs and how a person's beliefs may impact the results they have in life.

Sally has the following beliefs:

- Money doesn't grow on trees
- I must work hard for my money
- Money doesn't come easily
- Everyone has debt
- Credit card debt is a normal part of life
- Everyone struggles financially
- Money is hard
- Time is money
- People who have money just got lucky
- People who have money are greedy assholes
- Investing is for rich people
- Investing is gambling and for people who can "afford to lose money"

These beliefs reflect the money mindset that struggling financially in life is necessary and normal for you, that you must always work hard to make money, and you may even stray from wanting to save or invest because you believe it's scary. You also believe debt is normal, so having debt is within your comfort zone. You unconsciously don't want to be a "rich asshole," so having money might feel foreign or even wrong to you.

For a long time, I fell into the trap of having similar beliefs and a shared money mindset with Sally. I watched my parents work demanding jobs that left them exhausted at the end of the day, only to feel like they never truly "had enough." I can't remember a time when money wasn't a concern in our household. Except for a select few, it felt like most of the people in my life were in a similar situation: working hard, but always having too much month left at the end of their money. It felt like that was the way of life for people like me. While I could maybe change the situation a little bit, I'd always be someone who would live paycheck to paycheck and rely on credit cards to bridge the gap. Before I learned to rewrite those rules, I never focused on saving, because I didn't believe there was anything that could truly change my situation. So why save? I felt a weird sense of comfort in the struggle because *it was the norm for myself and those around me*—until I realized I had the power to change it all.

Fred has slightly different beliefs:

- Money is easy
- Money is abundant—if I don't have some now, I'll get some later
- There is good debt and bad debt; I avoid bad debt
- People with money have figured out a way to build wealth
- People who have done something I want to do worked to figure out how and didn't rely on luck
- If it's been done before, it can be done again
- People who have money have learned effective wealth management
- Investing is how you get rich
- Investing is a necessary tool for building wealth and creating financial security
- Everyone needs financial security
- Money isn't happiness, but everything takes money

These beliefs reflect a money mindset that money is less of a concern in life for you because you actively seek out ways to earn, save, and invest that are outside the norm. If you don't have money right now, it's because you haven't figured out how to get it yet. You strongly believe that, just because you haven't figured out a way to do something yet, that doesn't mean you can't do it—it just means you won't know how until you learn. Saving and investing are priorities for you because you believe they are the true path to building wealth, and financial security is extremely important.

While you know nothing about these people, you can see how their beliefs could shape their choices, and how those choices and decisions could impact the results they have in their lives. It's not like we're actively choosing which rules to listen to each day, because we're not consciously thinking about these things while we're choosing our paths in life. The majority of our day, we're in our subconscious (some sources even indicate this number can be as high as 95 percent), on autopilot, not actively thinking about what we're doing.[33, 34]

Ever drive home and wonder how you made it there because you don't remember the trip? It's because your brain went into autopilot mode. It does this when it's in a situation it's been in before, and it knows the rules to follow to get the job done. You don't actively think about which route to take; you likely just take the same one home, following the same pattern or set of rules. Your brain sees situations like this as opportunities to conserve energy, so you leave your conscious brain where active thought happens and go into the subconscious mind to let your predetermined rules and beliefs take over. Again, perhaps 95 percent of your day is spent here, in the subconscious, on autopilot,

---

33 gailmarrahypnotherapy.com/9-interesting-facts-about-your-subconscious-mind/
34 cambridge.org/core/journals/behavioral-and-brain-sciences/article/homing-in-on-consciousness-in-the-nervous-system-an-actionbased-synthesis/2483CA8F40A087A0A7AAABD40E0D89B2

not actively choosing your destiny, but relying on your internal rules and scripts to get you through the day.

Most of our actions during any average day are not intentional. They're predetermined. This is why it's so important to first discover your internal money beliefs and rules, and then to rewrite these beliefs and rules in such a way that they help you achieve your dream life. Until you do this, you will stay stuck.

UNCOVERING YOUR INTERNAL BELIEFS ABOUT MONEY

Do you want to uncover your internal beliefs about money and how they could be impacting your life today? Revealing the beliefs, scripts, and rules that make up your money mindset requires self-exploration, self-reflection, self-inquiry, and being honest and vulnerable with yourself.

To gain insight into your money mindset, write down and work through the following questions. Take your time thinking through your responses, and record any thoughts that arise as you progress through each question. There is no right or wrong answer. The goal here is to explore!

1. What did you hear from friends, family, or acquaintances about money growing up?

2. What do you think about: Saving? Earning/making money? Debt? Investing?

3. Do you have a story from childhood that stands out to you when you think about money? What happened? How do you think this experience contributed to your belief system about money?

4. What negative or limiting beliefs (beliefs that limit you or your potential in some way) do you hold about money? Write down each negative or limiting belief.

5. How might your negative or limiting beliefs about money be impacting your ability to achieve your long-term or dream life goals?

CHALLENGING NEGATIVE MONEY BELIEFS

Challenging negative money beliefs starts with acknowledging your negative money beliefs (see question four above).

Then, once you've identified your negative beliefs about money, you must do some research to prove yourself wrong. The best way to break down your money beliefs and rewrite them for success is to challenge your beliefs with contrary evidence.

For example, if your money belief is *All rich people are assholes*, you could come up with evidence that shows how people can and have used money for good. You could also come up with information that showcases the fact that money doesn't change people but magnifies who they already were instead. You could also compile a list of people without money who fit the *asshole* criteria.

Finally, after you record contrary evidence to discredit each of your negative beliefs about money, then you must positively reframe each belief to benefit you in achieving long-term success that aligns with your true happiness.

An example of a reframed belief is: *Money is a magnifier. It magnifies who I already was before having money, and is a medium that can be used to do good in the world and help me reach my dream life.*

Your newly reframed beliefs then become your replacement beliefs as you positively reshape your money mindset to support your plan for the future.

Three Steps to Challenging Negative Money Beliefs

1. Write down each negative or limiting belief you have about money (or revisit your notes on the beliefs you wrote down from our previous exercise).

2. Write down three examples of contrary evidence that proves each belief is wrong.

3. Positively reframe each belief to better serve or benefit you in reaching your dream life goals.

EXTERNAL BELIEFS ABOUT MONEY: A CURRENCY OF TIME

In addition to holding beliefs and rules about money and our lives, we also hold beliefs and rules about money in and of itself.

What is money? There are many potential answers to that question. Money is currency. Money is value. Money is a medium of exchange. While all are true, not all money is accepted by everyone everywhere, and not all money holds the same value or capacity for exchange. I was introduced to this concept through Vicki Robbins's book *Your Money or Your Life*, which has become a cult classic in the FIRE Community (Financial Independence Retire Early).

In her book, Vicki explains that, if we search for a definition of money that holds true for each one of us, we find that money is the physical result of time we've traded or sold. Most of us focus on trading our time for money—our hours for dollars—so money is a physical representation of the hours of our lives (averaging approximately 700,000 per person).

That five-dollar bill in your purse, that hundred dollars in your bank account, your paycheck—what do they all have in common? They all came from you selling hours of your life. Each is your compensation for giving up some of your most precious resource: time. Making this distinction is so important to changing the way we think about and view our money. We all have a finite amount of time we get to live. Our hours on this earth are numbered. If we are always trading hours for dollars, then we are effectively using little slivers of our lives to pay for the things we buy. This is also why it's so important to learn how to invest, so you can make money without your own physical input because your money can work harder than you ever could.

Ask yourself, truly, how do you see the money you have when you're spending it? Are you assigning the value to it that it really encompasses? It may seem like you are when you're at the checkout counter buying another pair of *super cute* shoes (you don't need and probably won't wear), because you're thinking of money like numbers in an account. I want you to stop doing that. Instead, start seeing each dollar as a representation of part of your life you will never get back—a part of your life you traded and could have used to do something else.

This is about the time that I'll get the people who say, "But, Nicole, I LOVE my job." To that I say, great!

The reality is a lot of people love a lot of things, and when you love something, generally, you're happy to spend money on it. So answer me this:

- Would you work completely for free at your job, since you love it so much?

- Would you *pay* to go to work?

If you answered no to one or both questions, then you don't *love* it as much as you think you do. Most people, if given the choice, would ultimately like to choose how they spend their time—and given the choice, would spend it doing something other than work.

So you're trading hours of your life working so you can get money, instead of doing something that truly makes you happy. Then you're using that money to buy crap that sits in the back of your closet. It's time to end that vicious cycle. It's going to feel scary and overwhelming, but anything worth doing is typically accompanied by a bit of fear. Part of feeling afraid comes from not having the proper tools. So let's get you equipped. The first step to getting you equipped is mastering the basic money rules.

CHAPTER 5

BASIC **MONEY** RULES

I used to think personal finance needed to be difficult, that it was complicated, and that's why so many people were struggling. There were too many things to think about, too many things to know, and a lot of being good with money just depended on luck (or where you came from and how many handouts you had from the bank of Mom and Dad).

This idea that personal finance was difficult actually came from my belief that a person couldn't really change their situation with money *that much.* Sure, you could go to school, make a little more, become more comfortable, buy more things, but you'd probably always struggle in some capacity. I believed the wealthiest I could ever be was middle-class (and there's nothing wrong with that). I believed that having real financial freedom just wasn't in the cards for me. I simply wasn't one of the *lucky ones.*

Where I grew up, there was quite a divide in terms of economic classes. There were people living in true poverty, people in the middle class, and people who were extremely rich (think mansions on acreage, hockey rinks in their basements, and regular business trips to Japan). I had friends who fit into each socioeconomic class, and I remember always feeling less-than when I went over to some of the houses of my "richer friends." Their families were eating okra soup for dinner and having flan for dessert, whereas frozen meatballs, white rice, and canned corn was a staple at my house.

It felt weird to me to see people flourishing with money. For a time, I lived with one of my close friends while I was in high school (my home life was tumultuous, so I didn't always stay there). I remember her dad always packing us a lunch. I don't think my friend ever realized this, but I couldn't believe her dad had the money to make her a sandwich (which he put in a new paper bag *every* day) and to make me one, too—on good bread, with good meat. From what I could tell, these rich friends who had rich families also had rich extended families. It wasn't like they were the anomaly. They were the norm where they came from.

After some soul-searching, I realized this idea of "difficult" really came from me watching the people in my life struggle with money. I internalized the notion that you either had money or you didn't, and if you weren't one of the lucky ones who did, you were doomed to struggle forever. For many years I felt stuck, trapped, and hopeless—none of which are great places to be. I didn't see a lot of people in my close personal life who were wealthy or financially successful, so I started to believe personal finance and money would always be difficult for me—this is known as complexity bias.

COMPLEXITY BIAS

Complexity bias is when we believe something is made up of many parts and is hard to understand because we innately find it easier to face a complex problem than a simple one. We quite literally prefer complicated explanations over simple ones. This can be due to our internal beliefs or societal pressures.

It's like, when you work something up in your head into this *big* problem that you have no idea how to solve, but then you get the solution and you're like, "Oh, that's it? Why didn't I think of that?" It's not because it was hard or difficult. It's because our brains can have a hard time believing something so life-changing can be so simple. Think of all the ways budgeting overcomplicates things by trying to fit each one of your expenses into a neat little "percentage of your income" box and forcing you to decide where each one of your "limited dollars" will go in advance. Think of all the times you believed you weren't good with money because you weren't good with math. When you thought you just weren't smart enough or skilled enough to make it work. In actuality, money is so innately simple—the tactics and what to physically do with it are easy. You can quite literally change your entire life just by following the rules in this chapter.

If money is so easy, why are so many people struggling? It's the aspects of internal psychology, behavior, and mindset that make money more difficult to master. Why? Because, although each one of these rules is simple, you need to follow them to see the change (hence the behavior and mindset components). Most of us have known what we need to do on some level for some time, but we haven't done it—even though we keep seeking out more and more tactical knowledge, searching for that complex explanation, instead of looking internally to figure out why we aren't implementing what we know.

Remember: Step 1 to changing your life is admitting something needs to change. Step 2 is learning what you need to change it, and Step 3 is actually *implementing* those changes in your life.

So what's happening internally that's keeping us stuck? Let's talk about the Mindless Dilemma.

THE MINDLESS DILEMMA

Most of us are going through life thinking each day is a new day, we are "starting fresh," when really you're just reliving the same day repeatedly. It's like *Groundhog Day*, where we wake up thinking today is different, but as soon as our feet hit the floor, it's like a time loop. While there may be small deviations in each day, just as in the movie, real change doesn't happen in the world—it happens within you. But it takes time and the ability to overcome your ego to realize the same mindless shit that got you where you are today isn't going to get you where you want to go. If you want different, you have to do different—and if you're reading this book, I think you're probably realizing where you're at right now isn't exactly where you want to be, so you need to change your behaviors to get there.

Even so, many of us will mindlessly continue to go through our days. Hoping, wishing, praying for a change, without ever making the choice to do something about it. We keep waiting to *feel* ready to do something about it. We are waiting for the motivation to come, so we can finally devote ourselves to change. People ask me all the time, "Nicole, how do you stay so motivated? How do you get up and continue to work toward your goals?" I'll let you in on a little secret: It's not motivation. It's being really clear about my goals and my dream life and getting up to do the damn thing even when I don't feel like it because my goals are more important than my feelings. I am in relentless pursuit of my goals 80 percent of the time, and the other 20 percent of the time, I allow myself to be human. However, if I always waited to feel motivated before taking action, I would not be where I am today.

Pro Tip: Being ready isn't a feeling. It's a decision. If you keep waiting until you feel like you're ready, you're going to miss out on all life has to offer.

Now we have ourselves a dilemma: If the majority of our days are spent on autopilot, meaning 80 to 90 percent of the time we are not actively choosing what we are going to do, we're just doing what we've always done, then we are destined to keep living the same day over and over, walking through life mindlessly.

Mindlessly spending money.

Mindlessly doing the same shit we've done every day that's gotten us where we are now.

Mindlessly throwing away a few dollars here and there because we believe:

1. Everyone does it.

2. A few dollars never changed anyone's life.

What if you are wrong? What if this mindlessness and this dilemma of wanting to do things differently, but moving through life mindlessly, was you letting life happen to you, instead of actively choosing your destiny?

To illustrate this point, let me remind you of Einstein's definition of insanity: "doing the same thing over and over and expecting different results."[35] Here's a shocker: The actions you take each day are why you're stuck with money, and in a lot of cases, your small habits could be keeping you broke.

I know. I know. I hear it already:

> "Oh, damn! I'm putting the book down because I cannot hear another person tell me to stop buying lattes and avocado toast."

> "Those are my only small pleasures in the day."

> "I don't spend that much." (Although, in my experience, most people are spending a *lot* more than they think they are because they're doing it mindlessly.)

> "You only live once, might as well enjoy it."

---

35   scientificamerican.com/article/einstein-s-parable-of-quantum-insanity/

Listen, I get it. If you *love* avocado toast, keep buying it. If you *love* Starbucks, keep buying it. If it brings you true happiness, enjoyment, and fulfillment, then keep buying it. Heck, spend more money on it, if it truly makes your heart skip a beat.

However:

- If you're just doing it out of habit, it needs to stop.

- If you're buying it without thinking, it needs to stop.

- If you're buying it simply because you're feeling too lazy to make a coffee at home, it needs to stop.

I'm not here to tell you what you can and cannot have, *but* if you continue to spend mindlessly out of habit, instead of coming from a place of intention every day—no matter how "small" these things are—you will unknowingly self-sabotage your goals.

Wondering how a simple coffee can be self-sabotage? First, remember, spending money is not the enemy—the enemy is spending out of alignment with your values and goals. Next, you need to know it's not about the coffee per se, but what the coffee represents. The coffee represents you creating the habit of spending money without bringing awareness to the transaction. Lastly, you also need to understand the opportunity cost because, as with everything in life, there is a tradeoff. We can't have *everything*, but maybe we can have what's most important to us.

If you spend just ten dollars a day on coffee and avocado toast (or insert another "small" daily purchase here), do you realize you could have been a millionaire in retirement instead? Without even realizing it, many of us are spending more than ten bucks daily on things we don't need, that don't bring us real joy or happiness, and that take us further away from our goals. If you saved and invested those ten dollars (key word: *invested*), instead of spending it, you could be a millionaire in forty years.

It's all about the opportunity cost. An **opportunity cost** is the cost of a lost opportunity—something you didn't get to do, have, see, or explore because you chose something else. Like an opportunity cost, everything in life is a tradeoff. You can have the coffee and avocado toast now, but maybe that means you can't go on a trip next year because you didn't plan and save for it. Choosing something today means not choosing something else in the future. When weighing tradeoffs, you must ask yourself, what's more important? There is no right or wrong answer here. The aim is to bring awareness to what we're doing.

Many times, we spend today without thinking about tomorrow. Yes, you're a priority today, but so is the person you'll be and the needs you'll have in the future. And it's time we start thinking about them, too. Maybe spending every dollar you make today feels good because #YOLO, but that could mean not saving for retirement. How will that lack of savings feel when you've got a few more decades under your belt? You can't buy a house because you're riddled with credit card debt and can't qualify for a loan (thanks to the few too many dollars you spent a "living your best life," even though not having a home is literally crushing your soul).

Weighing decisions between today and your future is like a simple game of "Would You Rather?"—it's truly not about the *things* we weigh against each other, but about what the things represent. It's about the Mindless Dilemma and how we go through life mindlessly spending and buying, thinking it makes us happy, yet being brought further and further from our real goals, and then complaining about not having what we want in life, like a house, a paid-off student loan, money in the bank, more time, more happiness, or financial freedom. We keep thinking we need to give up everything we love to get ahead with money, but we only need to give up the shit we keep spending on and don't care about.

So how do we determine if something is worth it to us or not? By bringing awareness to our daily routine, and questioning our actions to see if they're aligning with our true values and goals.

TRY THIS EXERCISE

To find out whether or not a purchase is worth it to you, I want you to first write down everything you've bought over the past week. Pull up your banking app, look at your credit card statement, and leave no stone unturned.

I want you to divide each purchase up into two categories, making a T table with one side for "Things that Improve My Life" and another side for "Things that Detract from My Life."

For the items you put under the improvement category, you're going to do four things:

1. Write down in what tangible way that purchase actually improved your life.

2. Write down another way you could have gotten that same benefit for less money (this is my WPM principle, more on that later).

3. Calculate how many hours you had to work for that expense, and note if there was something you would have rather done in that

time instead of working to pay for this item (like hanging out with your friends, going for a hike, or watching a funny movie).

4. Based on your responses, ask yourself if there are changes you'd like to make to that purchase in the future: Will you buy it again? If so, under what circumstances? Was there something else you could've gotten instead?

AWARENESS WITHIN YOUR DAILY ROUTINES

Once we know who we want to be, what our values are, and what our future goals are, it's time to bring awareness back to your daily routine. I want you to start questioning what you're doing, and seeing if your daily actions are in alignment with your values, goals, and who you ultimately want to be in life.

How do we bring awareness back into our daily routine?

· Be intentional about what you're spending—ask yourself, does this serve me, grow me, or make me truly happy? Do I already have something that fulfills this need or want?

· Be fully involved in what you're doing—be mindful of things you do that are out of habit, versus what you're doing because you truly want to be doing it.

· Start questioning what you're doing and why—I want you to take some time and write out your daily routine: what time you wake up, who you see, what you do, where you go, all that fun stuff. Then I want you to write out your dream life daily routine. Take some time to compare: Where are there differences, and what can you do to align the two?

· Are there things you're doing that bring you further from your goals, or don't align with your values? Consciously figure out a way to do it differently. For example, if you're buying coffee every day, but you realize this isn't in alignment with your values or goals and doesn't bring you true happiness, can you start making coffee at home instead? What can you do to rewrite your story?

· Write out your new daily schedule and dream life plan and refer back to it as you use it to form a new habit and internal life rules.

THE ONLY SEVEN MONEY RULES YOU NEED FOR FINANCIAL SUCCESS

When I started my personal finance journey, and I began to spend more time figuring out a different way of doing things than what tradition and society tell you to do, I realized that personal finance was simple. The "rules" of good personal finance were not difficult at all, but they were quite different from what society and school told us to do. Learning this easy set of rules could provide incredible success for anyone who followed them, without having to give up everything you love or restrict yourself with a budget. Yes, truly anyone. Now I'm here to share them with you.

Are you ready to change your freaking life? Here they are.

Seven "Rules" of Good Personal Finance

1. Live on less than you make.

2. Pay your future self first.

3. Buy only what brings you true happiness and fulfillment, closer to your goals, or serves you.

4. Invest early and often.

5. Plan for the unexpected.

6. Put your money where it will work the hardest for you.

7. Why Pay More (WPM Principle)

Yup, that's it! It really does get to be that simple.

Following these rules will provide you with the ability to:

- Maintain a good credit score

- Pay off your debt and keep it off, or steer clear of it in the first place

- Be prepared for emergencies

- Save for your future

- Make money while you sleep

- Feel confident in your financial situation

In fact, many of our students have found that following this simple set of rules provides them with more money than they ever thought possible, even though they never had to make drastic changes in their lives. They can save, pay off debt, and start investing—all without a budget and without making more money.

RULE ONE: LIVE ON LESS THAN YOU MAKE

Rule one is as simple as they come: Live on less than you make. Still, it's something so many of us struggle with. Now, undoubtedly, there are people in this world who, through engaging in full-time employment, are not able to get by—poverty is a real thing, and I'm not denying that. However, many of us believe our circumstances are fixed, and the paycheck-to-paycheck cycle we're stuck in is beyond our control. Many times, it is not.

There is a big difference between living in poverty and being broke. When you are living in poverty, there is something external preventing you from achieving economic certainty and prosperity. Things like low wages, social inequality, lack of access to education, or political instabilities can externally impact your ability to thrive economically. When you are broke, you may feel similar stressors to those living in poverty (not having enough money to pay bills, going into debt, feeling trapped), but the distinction is that through your actions, you've put yourself there.

Many of us choose to live beyond our means. We indulge in consumerism, by taking on a "buy now, pay later" lifestyle that can be challenging to break out of because we have already spent tomorrow's dollar (and in many cases, the dollars for a lot of days to come). According to Experian, in 2020, consumer debt in the US grew by almost 6 percent over the course of a year, which was the highest growth seen in over a decade.[36] The

---

36   experian.com/blogs/ask-experian/research/consumer-debt-study/

problem that prevents many people from living on less than they make is that society thrives on instant gratification and confuses true self-love and care with spending money frivolously in the name of "enjoying today" and "treating ourselves."

Ultimately, the idea that buying things brings us happiness just doesn't pan out long-term, especially when we buy things that provide us with only a short burst of dopamine—like when we impulse-buy a new "thingamajig" on Amazon, versus the fulfillment we get after an afternoon laughing with our friends or family. The joy we get out of spending money to consume material things doesn't make us happy, and studies confirm it.[37] I know you've been there (at the mall or scrolling on social media) and you've seen *the thing*. The thing you just absolutely must have right now. The thing that's going to *change your life, make it complete*, or *turn you into the person you've always wanted to be.* Many times, we buy things because we want the associated perception that comes along with owning the things, not necessarily because we want the things themselves.

To encourage this desire, good marketers don't sell products or talk about features. They sell an experience or lifestyle they want you to believe comes with ownership of *the thing*. Lululemon doesn't sell clothes. They sell you on the person you'll be when you own their clothes: healthier, through your mind, body, and soul. Apple doesn't sell electronics. They sell you on who you'll be when you buy their products: trendier, cooler, cutting-edge. Disney doesn't sell tickets to a theme park. They sell you on a dream, connecting with your children (or inner child), love, magic, and happiness. When we're scrolling on social media and see yet another person with the newest whatever-it-is, we don't just think about buying it because we want that thing, we think about buying it because we want the lifestyle that we believe

---

37   newdream.org/the-high-price-of-materialism-further-reading

comes along with it. We want to appear more successful, be seen as more attractive, perceived as cooler ánd as having it all together, which makes it even more difficult to say no. Instead, we're tempted to provide further justification for buying something we don't need that won't bring us real happiness, even though we believe it will on some inner level.

THE FIVE WHYS

The biggest changes and successes I've seen in my students have undoubtedly been when they dig deep and uncover the real reasons why they're purchasing things. An easy way to reveal this is by doing a root cause analysis using the Five Whys.

To get started, you will identify a statement or action you're trying to understand more deeply. Then, you will ask "Why?" five times to help dig down to the root cause that's motivating the action within you.

I'll use a personal example of a root cause analysis I've done for myself in the past to illustrate how it works:

Statement: I will only buy brand-name handbags.

1. *Why?*
   Because brand-name handbags are the only ones I like.

2. *Why?*
   Because I feel good when I use brand-name handbags.

3. *Why?*
   Because brand-name handbags make me look good, and when I look good to other people, I feel good.

4. **Why?**

   Looking good in the eyes of other people is important to me, so I can prove my worth and success.

5. **Why?**

   Because, for some reason, I'm not feeling worthy on my own, and I believe that I somehow gain worth and value by purchasing something that not everyone has.

Pro Tip: Now is not the time to phone it in. While you're going through this exercise, it can be tempting to self-sabotage and provide surface-level answers, or answers you think sound good but prevent you from digging deep and understanding your real internal motivations.

Remember, your ego is not going to like this. Depending on how much your ego interjects in the Five Whys process, you may have to complete a few attempts before you actually uncover the root cause of your action.

For example, after the second *why*, it would have been easy for me to say, "Well, I buy the name-brand handbags because they're better quality" and end it there, playing it off like that's the truth. An important reminder here is that, just because a statement is a true statement, that doesn't mean it's *your* true statement. You can also have a thought that's just a thought and not *your* truth.

Now, once you have the statement for your fifth *why*, you should have a better understanding of your underlying motivations. Awareness is the first step. It likely means you have unknowingly uncovered another internal money rule or script that has been running your life. When you uncover the money rules and scripts you've been living by, you can begin to dissect them to see if they align with who you want to be, based on whether it's helping you get closer to the life you want (or further away from it).

If you're struggling to rewrite the internal money rules you have that are not serving you when it comes to overspending, it is helpful to review some of the reasons why material things will never actually bring you true happiness.

1. There will always be something newer, nicer, better, or more expensive. When you're constantly chasing the high of the next and best, you're never complete, and you're always searching for more.

2. Many times, you believe purchasing *things* brings happiness into your life. Instead, those things bring you more stress than momentary joy. A new car becomes something you have to pay for each month and maintain, new clothes become clutter in the back of your closet, a new financed TV becomes something you need to trade more hours of your life for, instead of spending them actively enjoying life. (And if you went into debt to purchase any of these items, you've also now traded your happiness and security of tomorrow for your short-term fulfillment of today.)

3. Someone else will always have more than you. Like #1, someone will always have something newer, nicer, better, or more expensive.

4. The people you are unknowingly trying to impress don't care about your things as much as you think they do. Everyone is so focused on themselves and what everyone else is thinking about them that they usually don't have time to think about you. Meanwhile, you are ignoring what would truly bring you personal *real* happiness.

The key to living on less than you make is to only spend what you have available and to plan for the future, while understanding your triggers and motivations to overspending so you can begin to break those down and stop letting them run your life.

Our Five Whys allows us to get to the bottom of our spending motivations, but what are spending triggers, how do we identify them, and how do we control them?

Simply put, a spending trigger is any situation or emotion that tempts you to spend money—money you likely wouldn't have spent, had this circumstance not come up. We've all been there: spending more than we wanted to, or planned to, because something inside of us responded to a stimulus that told us to buy. There are thousands of possible triggers, but let's break them down into four main categories:

1. Perceived value

2. Keeping up with the Joneses

3. Buy now pay later

4. Filling an emotional void

PERCEIVED VALUE

The trigger of perceived value is when we see a sale, or a discount, and that prompts us to make a purchase we weren't previously intending on making. Like when you open your email inbox and see a flash sale for your favorite brand, so you justify to yourself that it's okay to make this purchase of something you didn't really need (and maybe didn't even really want) in the name of saving money.

Remember: there's no such thing as spending money on something you don't need to save money.

A great way to overcome this trigger is to limit your exposure—unsubscribe from email lists and unfollow accounts on social media that tempt you to buy things you don't want or need.

KEEPING UP WITH THE JONESES

Raise your hand if you've ever bought something because "everyone has it." Because it's the "next and best." Because you're worried about how you might be perceived if you don't "get it."

I remember this feeling of unworthiness creeping up in middle school—when all my friends started wearing brand-name clothing, and twelve-year-old me was trying to convince my mom that the reason she should buy me a forty-nine-dollar T-shirt was because of the *quality* (not the fact that every girl in my class had one, and I wanted to fit in).

I distinctly remember a day in eighth grade when I was wearing a pair of jeans I'd had for a few seasons that happened to be completely out of style. My mom kept telling me there was no need for new clothes because I already had so many, and that she wouldn't buy me any new ones until I started actually wearing the ones I had. So I took the plunge and wore these last-season, '70s-style jeans, in an attempt to prove to her that I was making use of what I had. These jeans were horrible—a weird kind of blue/green denim with overly flared bottoms (not the cute skinny jeans that were in style at the time). Just thinking back, I actually don't see how they were *ever* "in style," but they somehow ended up as one of my only options that day for pants.

I remember sitting at my desk, trying *so* hard to keep my ankles crossed under my chair, so no one could see the bottom of my pants (what I thought was an absolute fashion abomination). No one said a single thing about my jeans that day, but I spent the entire eight hours in school feeling flushed and anxious that someone would "spot" me. That someone would see I wasn't as cool as they were.

It was this day that I decided I would no longer be "that girl." Even though I wasn't "that girl" to anyone else but myself.

This, and a few other events, laid the groundwork for me getting a job at twelve and using the majority of that money for expensive clothing so I could "look the part."

Keeping up with the Joneses is as much about not feeling left out as it is about the fear of being singled out or "found out."

The key for me in overcoming this trigger was getting a clear understanding of who I actually wanted to be, working on my self-limiting beliefs, understanding that I was worthy with or without the "stuff," finding out what real happiness and my true dream life looked like, and learning not to give a f*ck about what anyone else thought of me.

BUY NOW PAY LATER

This is one of the most insidious triggers, because not only do you end up stealing from future you to pay for things you want today, but you could be paying a premium for it.

In the case of using credit cards to fund your purchases, you could be paying upwards of 19–24.99 percent interest. You may think to yourself, "It's fine, I'll pay it off at the end of the month," but 55 percent of Americans say they carry a credit card balance from month to month.[38]

On average, Americans are carrying $6,194 in credit card debt.[39]

---

38 finance.yahoo.com/news/jaw-dropping-stats-state-credit-130022967.html
39 cnbc.com/select/average-credit-card-balance-by-state/

If you were to pay the minimum balance of 3 percent ($185.82 a month), with a 24.99 percent interest rate, it would take you fifty-eight months to pay off. In this time, you would end up paying over $4,487 in interest, making your credit card bill of $6,194 actually cost you $10,681 (almost double).

Credit Card Balance

$ 6,194

Credit Card Interest Rate

24.99%

Payment Per Month

$ 185.82

YOUR RESULT

Total Principal Paid	$6,194
Total Interest Paid	$4,487

Monthly Payment	Months to Payoff
$185	58

58% Principal	42% Interest
$6,194	$4,487

The first step in overcoming this trigger is understanding that using a buy now pay later service or credit card to make a purchase means that you are essentially taking out a loan.

So if you're putting a pitcher of margaritas at the bar with your friends on a credit card because you don't have the cash, I want you to say out loud to yourself: "I'm taking out a loan to buy a pitcher of margaritas."

If you're buying a sweater you don't need on buy now pay later, I want you to say out loud: "I'm taking out a loan to buy a sweater."

Doesn't feel good saying it? Use this as the opportunity to bring awareness back to what you're actually doing.

Another helpful measure is to start leaving your cards at home, and delete your credit card information from your phone and computer to make it more difficult to make impulse purchases.

FILLING AN EMOTIONAL VOID

Lastly, this category is a catch-all for any emotion that causes you to feel the temptation of spending. These emotions might include jealousy, happiness, envy, stress, sadness, anxiety, or fear.

When something happens to us, or inside of us, whether good or bad, it can cause a feeling or void that we may decide to fill with a purchase.

Ever had a bad day at work and stopped on your commute home to do some shopping?

Ever had a *great* day at work, and went out to celebrate by...shopping?

Ever been bored at work, so you end up spending your time... shopping online?

Emotional spending can be a catch-all solution for any kind of feeling. Here are some tips on how to recognize when it's happening and curb the habit.

1. Before you go to purchase something, ask yourself: Is it necessary, do I need this, do I already have something that fills this need? Take an inventory of how you're feeling right now (anxious, happy, sad, overwhelmed). Ask yourself if you truly want/need the item, or if there is potentially something else going on. (You can use the Five Whys here!)

2. Put some space between yourself and the purchase—keep it in your cart if you're online shopping, write it down somewhere, and set a reminder for yourself to come back in seven to ten days. If you've forgotten about the item, or your life is no different because of not having it, then that can be a sign that you may not want to make that purchase.

3. Work out how many hours of your life you'd have to trade to buy the item—take the cost of the item, divided by your hourly wage (calculate this based on how many hours you *actually* work, and what your *take-home* pay is, i.e., after taxes and expenses are taken out).

For example, let's say you make twenty dollars an hour take-home, and the sweater you want is a hundred dollars. That would mean you would need to work five hours for that sweater. Does that feel good to you? Does that feel in alignment with your values, goals, and dream life? If not, that could be a sign that this isn't the right purchase for you.

TWO COMPONENTS OF LIVING
ON LESS THAN YOU MAKE

When it comes to living on less than you make, I know that can seem easier said than done—especially if you've already gotten into the habit of borrowing from your future self to pay for expenses today (through the use of credit cards or payday loans, for example).

There are two main components that I've identified throughout my own financial independence journey, and through helping students of our programs, as the main factors for success in living on less than you make.

1. The tactics: what accounts to use, and how to physically manage your money

2. The behavior and psychological component (the mental foundation required for the tactics to work): overcoming self-sabotage and moving into alignment with your values, goals, and who you want to be in life

Step 1 is what everyone wants—Step 2 is what everyone needs.

People love to skip out on Step 2, because it's actually the harder part— where you have to confront the fact that, even though many times we know what we're supposed to do to change our situation (save more, pay off debt, start investing), we aren't doing it. All the tactics in the world (learning the best accounts to use, the winning investment strategy, the best ways to pay off debt) won't help you if you don't address the mindset stuff...because you just won't put it all into action long-term.

TACTICS

The first step to living on less than you make is to organize your finances.

If you're anything like I was before my financial literacy journey, you have a checking account that your pay gets deposited into, and your bills and expenses get paid out of. Your savings are nothing more than money that is sometimes left over in your account before your next paycheck hits.

Or maybe you have a savings account, but there isn't a specific goal you've been saving for or strategy you're using to manage that money:

the account works a little more like a revolving door of good intentions and inefficient planning, where you transfer money over when you're feeling good about your financial situation, but by the next month or so, you're dipping back into it to pay for something today.

Even though this is a common way to set up your money, it's inefficient; it can cause you to unknowingly overspend and prevent you from actually hitting your savings goals.

The way we are going to set up our finances is through something I call the Bare Four, where you have at *minimum* four accounts, each one serving a separate purpose.

The Bare Four accounts are:

- Checking account

- Two high-yield savings accounts

- Retirement account

The first account in the Bare Four is your checking account. This is your standard, run-of-the-mill account that you use to receive your pay (paychecks get deposited here) and pay your expenses from.

This can be opened at any financial institution, but a few things to look out for are: the fees (obviously we want to pay the least amount possible for this account), the inclusions (are there things you use on a regular basis, like ATMs or cashier's checks? How much do they cost to use, what is their availability?), the reputation (do they have good customer service?), whether they're insured (so your money is protected—FDIC-insured in the US and CDIC-insured in Canada), and what kind of access they provide to your money (apps, online banking, in-person services).

I personally like to keep about five to six weeks' worth of bare-bones expenses in this account.

What's a bare-bones expense? Think of the things you most absolutely *have* to pay for, such as rent or mortgage, phone bill, car loan, and insurance payments.

If you don't have five to six weeks' worth of expenses available to put in this account right now, *don't worry*. The purpose isn't to have everything done on day one—this is a marathon, not a sprint. You are here learning the strategies to use to change your financial situation: this doesn't mean everything is going to be ready to go today, but it does mean that every day, moving forward, you are going to take steps in the right direction to help you start building that dream life.

Every dollar saved is a dollar saved. Every step in the right direction is a step in the right direction—no matter how "small." Rome wasn't built in a day.

The second account in the Bare Four is your high-yield savings account (HYSA). The best ones are typically through online financial institutions, because they usually offer better savings rates (so you're making more money on your money just by putting it in the right place). This is because they don't have physical locations to pay for, so they're able to pass those savings along to their clients. If you're technologically savvy, then using an online bank shouldn't be a problem—in my experience they're super user-friendly, and easy to set up.

Our HYSA is going to be used for our emergency fund, and our short-term savings goals (think of anything less than five years out—like saving for a new car, or a down payment on a home).

We need to have at minimum two accounts opened so we can keep each savings goal separate. You can just open two accounts with the same provider—I personally use an online bank that allows me to open five accounts at no cost, so I can assign a different goal to each account.

Pro Tip: Name each of these accounts (you can usually do this in the settings section of your app or online banking platform) to reflect the goal you're saving for. You can use names like Emergency Fund, New Home, or even Trip to Bali! This way you stay organized, and it can psychologically prime you to keep saving as you see yourself getting closer and closer to your big win. This can also help prevent you from self-sabotaging and "stealing" from your goals to pay for shit you don't really need today—because it's a thousand times more powerful seeing the account named "new home" than "savings account."

To begin, you'll have two accounts: one for your emergency fund, and the other for your sinking fund.

We'll talk more about your emergency fund in Rule Five: Plan for the Unexpected. For now, know that this is an account you keep money in to help you in the event of an emergency, or unexpected expense, to prevent you from going into debt to pay for it.

Your sinking fund, on the other hand, is for big, short-term expenses you know are coming up, but need to save for. For example, if you know you're going to need new tires for your car next year, or you have an out-of-town wedding to go to, you can use this account for those savings. You may also choose to break those out into their own accounts in your HYSA—whatever makes more sense to you.

To figure out how much you need in the account, you're going to need to identify and then reverse-engineer your goal.

For example, let's say you need new tires next year. You do some research and figure they're going to cost you about six hundred dollars.

Next step is to decide on your timeline—when do you need to buy them?

Let's say it's twelve months away. Now we take our goal of six hundred dollars and divide it by twelve months, to see exactly how much we need to be saving each month—fifty dollars. The next step is to set up automatic transfers once a month from your checking account when you get paid, directly into the account set up for this savings goal. This way you know you are on track to having exactly what you need, when you need it.

The last account in the Bare Four is your retirement account. I know at this moment in time retirement might be the last thing on your mind, especially if you're working to get out of the paycheck-to-paycheck cycle—but I promise you, this is not something we can put off. The earlier you get started, the easier it will be for you—and if we sacrifice tomorrow for today, we're just kicking the can down the road. We will have to deal with it eventually, and it's so much less work (and takes *less money*—hello, major win) to start now.

We'll go over in detail how to start investing for your retirement, what accounts to use, and the best places to open them in chapter 9, but for now you can start thinking about the importance of building your future, not just your today (because tomorrow is coming, whether you like it or not).

My recommendation is to find your top three account or financial institution options for each category, and create a spreadsheet with all of the details so you can easily compare and find which one works best for you.

BEHAVIOR AND PSYCHOLOGY

How many times have you said, "I really should save more," "I should start paying my debt," or, "I should get to those bills," but you don't?

The problem many of you are facing is that, on some level, you know what you need to do. You know you "should be" doing an array of things that bring you closer to your true life goals, but you're not doing them. You're self-sabotaging. You're getting in our own way. You're the thing that's standing between you and the life you want—but no matter how hard you try to become "motivated," you don't end up having long-term success.

This problem is twofold: the first part is that you're relying on motivation to get you where you want to be.

If you want to see long-term success in life, you absolutely cannot rely on motivation. I'm successful today not because I'm more motivated than other people, but because I get up and do what needs to be done whether I'm feeling motivated or not. For context, I'm writing this section of the book on only a few hours of sleep after being up with a crying newborn all night (and I may or may not have a baby-vomit stain down the side of my shirt). I didn't wake up motivated to spend the morning writing, but I got up and did the thing, because that's what I need to do. That's what gets me closer to my goals. That's what helps me build my dream life.

When you can learn to get up and do the damn thing whether you feel like it or not, because you are so clear about who you want to be and what goals you want to achieve, that's when you'll find your success: when you decide you're going to be in relentless pursuit of your dream life.

The second part of the problem is that you're "shoulding" all over yourself.

"I *should* do this."

"I *should* do that."

Has anyone ever really been happy doing something that they "should do"? Just the language itself implies it's not your first choice, like there's something else you'd rather be doing.

"I should be saving this money"—instead of spending it on an impulse purchase.

"I should start paying down that debt"—instead of ordering another round of takeout.

And in my experience, a lot of this "shoulding" comes from the fact that we see financial responsibility as deprivation: Why would you save, invest, or pay down debt when the benefit is so far away?

Which brings us to our next rule—paying your future self first.

RULE TWO: PAY YOUR FUTURE SELF FIRST

How many times have you said something to the effect of, "If I had only done XYZ a year ago, I'd be so much better off right now"? When we're talking about money-related regrets, it usually boils down to wishing we had saved more to better prepare our future selves. For some reason, even though we know we should be setting our future selves up for success, many of us put our future selves last. We prioritize ourselves in the present without regard for our future selves and needs two years, five years, ten years, or more from now. The rule of paying your future self first aims to turn this on its head to ensure your future self is prepared to achieve all your life and financial goals with a little planning today.

How good does it feel to put on a jacket you haven't worn in over a year, only to find a crisp twenty-dollar bill in the pocket? Well, imagine this feeling multiplied by a thousand when your future self wants to go on vacation, buy a house, or pay for your wedding, and you have the cash to do it! Paying your future self first means, before you set aside money for anything else, you are going to pay your future self. Before paying yourself first, you must determine what your future self wants, both in the short and long term. Take some time to think about where you see yourself in two years, five years, and even ten years. What do you want for yourself? Once you figure that out, then you can pay them first. Set aside money for your goals before you put money into anything else.

Paying your future self first also means giving up the approach you likely take with your goals, which is hoping, wishing, and praying that one day you will get there. Instead, this rule forces you to look at your future goals now, reverse-engineer them, and figure out exactly what you need to be doing *today* to set yourself up for success in the future—so that you *will* be able to buy that house, pay for that wedding, or go on that trip. We'll talk exactly how to plan out these goals in another section, but for now, know that planning and thinking about your future is essential to being good with money.

Pro Tip: As human beings, we are prone to self-sabotage, the art of getting in our own damn way. To be successful with money, we want to automate as many things as possible and take our brain out of it. When we take our brain out, we can help prevent ourselves from actively choosing, and set ourselves up to just do the damn thing. When it comes to saving money, don't wait until your paycheck hits your checking account to decide how much you're going to save and then manually transfer it over—that only leaves room for you to potentially decide *Ahh no, I'm not going to do that this week*. Instead of sabotaging ourselves this way, we are going to automate those savings to happen *automatically*, without our input, at regular intervals.

AUTOMATE SAVING FOR YOUR FUTURE SELF

How do you do this? Follow the steps below to automate your saving.

1. Call your bank or use your banking app

2. Select the account the savings are going to come out of

3. Determine the amount that is going toward your goals

> This should always be a dollar amount, because we want our savings to be specific. I don't agree with the rhetoric that we should be saving a percentage of our pay for our goals, because the lack of specificity means we are taking a hoping/wishing approach to our finances. We hope to achieve this goal one day. But when we determine the specific dollar amount, we know exactly what we need to do and when, and can be sure we are on track to achieve it.

4. Determine the type of account that these savings should be in (are you investing the money for retirement, are you saving in a high-yield savings account to beef up your emergency fund? Each goal may call for a different type of account—we'll review these details shortly)

5. Set up automatic withdrawals from your account into the goal account—you can do this every pay period. Depending on your employer, you may also be able to arrange a split direct deposit, where the amount you've determined is going to your goals is directly deposited into the account(s) of your choosing by your employer (less work for you!)

Pro Tip: Use an online bank separate from your everyday bank for your short-term savings goals. You'll want to find a high-yield or high-interest account for your emergency fund and short-term goals, to be accomplished within five years or less. (When a goal is longer-term, more than five years out, that's when you may want to consider investing the money—but more on this later). Online banks are typically best for these accounts because they have lower costs and provide you higher interest. Using an online bank separate from your regular bank is beneficial because:

- It can prevent you from self-sabotaging, since the money isn't as easily accessible

- It can provide higher interest to fight inflation on your cash savings

- Depending on the bank, sometimes you can open multiple bank accounts and name them after your goals to keep you organized (hello #HouseFund or #BaliGirlsTrip), and it also prevents you from being tempted to steal from your future self for shit you don't need today

RULE THREE: BUY ONLY WHAT BRINGS YOU TRUE HAPPINESS AND FULFILLMENT, BRINGS YOU CLOSER TO YOUR GOALS, OR SERVES YOU

A quick caveat on this rule: Things like paying your bills, mortgage or rent, or a popped tire may not seem like payments that bring you true happiness or fulfillment, but these #adulting expenses will bring you closer to your goals of good financial management and an increased credit score, and they also serve you by providing you with things like transportation and shelter.

By fixing your popped tire, you can get to work, and you can have freedom of movement to go out, to see your friends and family.

By paying your bills on time, you get to work to increase your credit score, which could impact future goals like buying a house or new vehicle.

By paying your rent or mortgage, you have the ability to live in your own space, and have security of shelter.

I know it can feel crappy when money leaves your account for things you "have to" pay for, but it's important to keep in mind how these things all work together to provide you with personal and financial security.

Living on less than you make really hinges on this rule of buying only what brings you true happiness and fulfillment, or serves you. But what does this really mean? A lot of us mistakenly believe what we're buying makes us happy because we believe we feel happiness when we buy it. Is this happiness not *real* happiness? Let's explore it.

Looking at what different schools of thought teach about happiness helped me learn and understand its true meaning. Although the dictionary definition of happiness is "the state of being in joy,"[40] I didn't think that really encompassed all that happiness was, because so many of us live our lives in search of happiness and joy but are unable to truly find it. We seek positive emotions

---

40   merriam-webster.com/dictionary/happiness

and life satisfaction, as our national unhappiness ranks at its highest levels ever.

When I first started my personal finance journey, I went through what I call my "quarter-life crisis." I didn't understand what happiness was, how to get it, why we were all here on this earth, and what life even meant. I started reading books on philosophy, the meaning of life, and different takes on what it all means through the eyes of Buddhism and Stoicism.

LET'S TALK BUDDHISM

Buddhism is an ancient religion that focuses on achieving enlightenment, or an inner state of peace and wisdom.

WHAT DOES BUDDHISM SAY ABOUT HAPPINESS?

One of the books that stood out to me on happiness was a book titled, quite literally, *The Art of Happiness*, by the Dalai Lama (spiritual leader of Tibetan Buddhism). In the book, the Dalai Lama says that, in Buddhism, there is consistent reference to the four factors of fulfillment or happiness: adequate wealth, worldly satisfaction, spirituality, and enlightenment.[41]

There are a few things I want to break down from this:

1. He uses fulfillment and happiness interchangeably—and according to Merriam-Webster, "fulfillment" is synonymous with "satisfaction, or to be satisfied." In our gluttonous society, we typically consume past the level of satisfaction into overconsumption (I'm looking at you, all-you-can-eat buffets).[42]

---

41   pdx.pressbooks.pub/thebalanceofpersonality/chapter/happiness-the-science-of-subjective-well-being/
42   merriam-webster.com/dictionary/fulfillment

2. He says that there are four factors to fulfillment, meaning in this context that simply obtaining material goods in and of itself can't bring true happiness, because it takes multiple factors to achieve and buying something is just one. Materialism is what accounts for the temporary happiness we feel when we buy things, but the reality is that materialism has no significant lasting impact on total life satisfaction, positive feelings, or low negative feelings/experiences.

3. Wealth is included in the definition of happiness, but the term he uses is "adequate wealth." What I take this to mean is that should you have enough wealth to satisfy you, to bring you to a feeling of fulfillment, to fulfill your basic needs, and a little more for comfort.

From a wealth and money perspective, Buddhism believes wealth is temporary and is not a path to happiness, and that suffering in life comes from our desires—always being in the position of wanting and needing. In the day-to-day context, Buddhism teaches us to let go of desire and greed to live simply, where we have the necessities to live a comfortable life, but no excess.[43]

WHAT DOES BUDDHISM SAY ABOUT WEALTH AND MONEY IN OUR DAILY LIVES?

There are five main lessons Buddhism teaches about wealth and money in our daily lives:

1. **Eat simple and healthy food.** It saves you money and helps with your health.

---

43   teachingsofthebuddha.com/Buddhism-and-Money

2. **Don't buy things you don't need.** If you buy things you don't need, you'll likely put yourself into debt and fail to have funds for the other important things in your life.

3. **Work not because of money, but for service.** If you're only working for money, you'll never be happy.

4. **Don't have vices.** If you're constantly hiding from stress or other unpleasant feelings, instead of processing them, you'll have a hard time finding your true happiness. Additionally, vices cost money that could be better spent going after positive feelings and goals, instead of hiding from negative ones.

5. **Share what you have.** Money is abundant; allow wealth to flow from you to help those in need.

While I agree with all those points, I think it's important to remind you again that spending money is not the enemy. However, the enemy is spending out of alignment with our values and goals. I've personally had positive experiences with each one of these lessons in my own life. When I focused on eating healthy foods at home instead of fast food and takeout, I was able to save more effortlessly, and my autoimmune condition benefited greatly. I discovered that the food I was eating correlated directly to my flares. When I stopped buying things I didn't need, I had more money for things that brought me true happiness, joy, and closer to my goals. When I stopped seeing work as my life and a way to make money, and instead a way to get myself and my family closer to freedom and our dream life, I began to enjoy it more. When I stopped using alcohol as a way to cope with my stress, I had more money in the bank, and a clearer mind to process my problems. When I focused on setting my friends, family, students, and community up for success alongside myself, the returns were endless.

LET'S TALK STOICISM

Stoicism is a "philosophy that was once one of the most popular civic disciplines in the West, practiced by the rich and the impoverished, the powerful and the struggling alike in the pursuit of the Good Life."[44] I was first introduced to stoicism in my college philosophy class, and one of the major things my professor said that stood out to me was that the stoic approach to life was "Meh," and he shrugged his shoulders as he said it—meaning they took things with a grain of salt and were *unbothered*. They had achieved a level of no f*cks given that so many others wish to embody.

WHAT DO THE STOICS SAY ABOUT HAPPINESS?

The Stoics believed perception is the basis of true knowledge; that what you believe becomes what you know, and that happiness comes from the pursuit of virtue. What does it mean to pursue virtue? The pursuit of virtue means becoming the best version of yourself, and to do this you must take personal responsibility for the state of your life.

According to *The Daily Stoic*, there are five stoic strategies you can implement to become a better, happier person:

1. **Stop worrying about what you can't control.** Things you can't control include what other people think about you, how you are perceived by others, and external events.

2. **Focus on what you can control.** Do not focus on what events have happened to you. Instead, focus on how you act and react to them (by taking radical responsibility for your life).

3. **Think about death.** Not in a morbid kind of way, but in more of a *Hey, I won't be here forever* kind of way. So if you're always trading time for

---

44   dailystoic.com/what-is-stoicism-a-definition-3-stoic-exercises-to-get-you-started/

money to buy things to impress people you don't really like (or know), then maybe that's a waste of your most precious resource.

4. **Want less.** Stop focusing on "wants" (listening to the ego speaking) and focus on finding joy with where you're at. Ever heard the saying, "Life is about the journey, not the destination"? If you're always focusing on what you want, that's focusing on lack and what you don't have—that will make you unhappy.

5. **Simplify your life.** This promotes minimal living, like the rule *Buy only what brings you true happiness and fulfillment, or serves you, and nothing more.*

PERMA PROFILER: A MEASURE OF HAPPINESS

What I found most interesting about the views on happiness by Buddhism and Stoicism was that they were closely in line with what science says about happiness as well. Martin Seligman, one of the founders of positive psychology, has created a way to measure happiness that he calls **PERMA Profiler**. Essentially, it's a tool used to determine if someone is *flourishing* and in psychological well-being (or in *happiness*).

PERMA stands for:

- **Positive Emotions**—including hope, interest, joy, love, compassion, pride, amusement, and gratitude. These emotions are the baseline that help people build the resources that create resilience and overall well-being.

- **Engagement**—is a byproduct of happiness, something that happens when you do something that really lights your fire. You become one with even the most boring parts of it, because you feel that connection.

- **R**elationships—these are the interactions you have with people in your life: friends, family, people at work, your neighbors. Having positive relationships and social connections within our personal communities is an integral part of happiness.

- **M**eaning—having a purpose in life, feeling connected to what you're doing on a daily basis can provide the ability to achieve greater life satisfaction.

- **A**ccomplishments—being able to not only work toward, but also achieve your goals. This can easily tie in with meaning (do you feel accomplished in your home and work life?).[45]

While many of us have created this belief that money and things equal happiness, the data and thought leaders say differently. According to them, the way to achieve happiness is to focus on becoming the best version of yourself, understanding what brings you satisfaction but not overindulgence, that happiness is not a single thing or something you can buy but a set of factors (like relationships and accomplishments). I also found that overall, the meaning of life, quite literally, was to live in happiness (a positive life experience) because without happiness, what do we have?

What I learned from this exploration is that money in and of itself is not happiness, but that it can provide happiness if used as a tool to build the life we truly want. For example, I don't find happiness today in the fact that *I'm a millionaire*. I find happiness in the freedom it provides me—the freedom for me to spend my limited time on this earth how I wish. I find happiness in the fact that I live life by my values, and I use my money as a tool to help me live by my values and achieve my goals.

---

45   positivepsychology.com/perma-model/

ALIGNING YOUR VALUES AND GOALS

The first step in learning how to do this for yourself is to understand your values. A **value** is something that is important to you. Everyone's values will be different, but it's imperative for you to understand your own, so you know if you are living life in a way that will truly help you find happiness—because that's the real point here, isn't it? Additionally, it's important to understand our values, as they should be in alignment with our goals. A goal that is not in alignment with your values is (although not impossible) much, much harder to achieve. By understanding their values, many people realize the reason they were "failing" to achieve certain goals is because those goals weren't aligned with what they truly wanted from life. Instead, the goals were aligned with what they thought they were "supposed to do" or what was expected of them by some external agent, like parents, family, society, friends, etc.

A lot of people seem to struggle with figuring out their values. Here's my advice for that:

1. **Think about who you want to be in life.** Do not focus on who you are right now, unless it feels good to you. If it doesn't, know you have the choice. We have thousands of versions of ourselves living within us, and by choice we become one version. Don't like where you are in life? Choose to be someone different. Not sure who that is? Think about someone you admire. What is it about them you admire? Is it the way they act? React? How they speak? How they treat others and themselves? Think about their actions, what's important to them, and what their values might be, and use this as a starting point to craft your own ideal.

2. **Think about the times when you feel most alive.** When you feel like you're flourishing, think about what values are being displayed during those times. Now think about times where you feel stifled, sad, or insecure. What values are being displayed in those times? This could be a good indication of what resonates with you personally.

Remember, there are no right or wrong answers here. This is all about what feels good to you.

3. **Use a resource to brainstorm your values.** Check out the list of values below to get an idea of what might be of value to you. If any others come to mind, feel free to add them to the list. Then, pick ten of the top values that are most important in your life.

WHAT DO YOU VALUE?

Freedom	Security	Faith	Clarity	Affection
Finances	Self-Respect	Safety	Loyalty	Intelligence
Connection	Family	Creativity	Wellness	Justice
Grace	Encouragement	Home	Beauty	Wisdom
Personal Development	Friendship	Leadership	Innovation	Honesty
Health	Fitness	Free Time	Career	Humility

4. **Narrow your list to your most important values.** Shorten your list of values down to your top five. Focus on those as the values you will use to run your life. This list of values will help you form the rules you use to make decisions so that, if you ever get into a situation and find yourself unsure of what to do, you can refer to your values. Ask yourself: *How does each potential decision align with or deflect from my values and what I truly want in life?* Allow your answers to lead your decision-making.

Pro Tip: What you think are your values right now may not be your true values. Many of us need to reevaluate our values and consider where they

MORE MONEY NOW

really came from. Do they come from us, or were they passed down to us through society, tradition, our family, or our friends? Before we decide to use those as the basis for decision-making in our lives, we must ensure they accurately reflect what's important to us.

For example, for a long time, I believed one of my major values was luxury. I often used this as an excuse to splurge on designer items, justifying it with *that's just who I am*. I even aligned my goals to this value. I wanted to work my way up the corporate ladder to make more money, so I could spend it on expensive cars, jewelry, clothes, and the lot. However, after taking time to do some introspection, I came to see that I didn't really want those things. I only thought I wanted them because I was told they were what I needed to be respected, liked, admired, and seen as successful. While I still like nice things that bring me joy, my focus has shifted from things that are unnecessarily expensive to things that get me closer to my ultimate values of family and freedom.

WHAT ARE YOUR VALUES AND GOALS?

As I mentioned earlier, yes, you can reach a goal that isn't consistent with your values, but it's harder. To reduce the difficulty, you need to get clear about who you want to be in your dream life, remembering that who you are right now is irrelevant and does not dictate what you get to have in life.

Use the values you came up with to help you determine your goals. How can you use money as a tool to get to your dream life and ultimately to get real happiness? If your goals are daunting or too big, break them down and reverse-engineer them to see what you need to do today to set yourself up for success in the future. Turn them into bite-sized pieces. Take some time to think about what you want your life to look like in one year, five years, and ten years. What can you do today that will set future you up for success?

Ask yourself how many times you have said, "I wish I had done XYZ because I'd be in a better spot right now," referring to something you did (or didn't do) to set yourself up for success today. Start planning for the future today and making your future self a priority—the you of today isn't the only one that matters

WHAT SERVES YOU?

There will undoubtedly be expenses in our lives we must pay for that won't bring us happiness, joy, or fulfillment, but we will have to pay for them anyway. This is where the last part of this rule comes in: buy what serves you. Expenses like rent, groceries, or new tires may not be the most exciting purchases to make, but they serve you. While they may not bring happiness directly, a roof over your head, food in your stomach, and the ability to drive safely lend themselves to feelings of happiness. Any expense that has a non-negotiable, essential purpose is considered an expense that serves.

RULE FOUR:
INVEST EARLY AND OFTEN

Since we're going to get into all the dirty details of investing later in this book, this brief introduction is just the basics. When it comes to investing, here's what's most important to know:

- Investing isn't *for* the rich. It's *how* you get rich.

- Investing is how you provide yourself with financial security.

- Investing is the best way to make more money because you don't have to trade hours of your life for it (this is how we make money while we sleep).

- Investing works and grows your money by contributing more money or by giving it more time to grow on its own (get that compound interest, baby!).

Pro Tip: When it comes to investing, **time is more valuable than money.** Let's look at a couple of examples:

Example One: If you invest $200 a month for forty years, you could end up with over $1,100,000—with $1,014,000 of that being *free* money (money you made without having to work for it).

Example Two: If you invest $400 a month for twenty years, you will only have $287,000—with $191,000 being *free* money (money you made without having to work for it).

In both examples, you contributed the same amount of money: $96,000. However, in the first example, you gave your investments more time to grow and work for you. Many people don't think they have the money to invest, but the reality is that, if you don't have a lot, that's okay, because time will work harder for you than your money does. As a result, investing early and investing often is key to financial success. (We'll teach you exactly how to do this in chapter 9.)

Until then, don't skip ahead! Remember, we're building your foundation right now, and without the foundation, you could put yourself in a position to *lose* money—and that's not what we want.

RULE FIVE: PLAN FOR THE UNEXPECTED

We think life is a series of random events we can't plan for, because *who can predict the future,* amirite? But even just knowing that life is a series of unexpected events means that life is in a way *predictable*. We know something unexpected will always arise. So if we know something is always likely to happen, that the shit somewhere, sometime, somehow will hit the fan, we can begin to plan for it.

Maybe we don't know exactly what's going to happen, but we know that something will happen. Whether it's your car breaking down, your cat needing to go to the vet, your roof leaking, or you losing your job—something will happen, so let's start to plan for it. Maybe you can't plan for the particulars because you don't know what those are yet, but my rule of thumb for protecting yourself from a financial standpoint against these events is having a catch-all emergency fund.

I grew up believing credit cards and lines of credit were emergency funds. They were the *Oh shit, this happened, and I didn't expect it!* fund. It was my understanding that they were literally meant to be used in the case of an emergency. However, through my personal finance journey, it became clear that this rule and belief is a great way to set yourself up for failure and to get stuck in a vicious cycle of debt that is difficult to break away from. I want to make something very clear here: Using debt to get you through a hard time is a good way to put yourself in a hard time in the future—but, of course, I understand that sometimes there is no other option.

Moving forward, however, you want to make sure you do have the option the next time something comes up. To do this, you start by saving a baby emergency fund of a thousand dollars. Then, you work up to saving three to six months' worth of bare-bones expenses, and eventually six to twelve months' worth. Tackling this task in steps helps to give you smaller goals to work toward over a period of time. Psychologically, this way of breaking down your goals allows the incremental success to help push you a little harder to get to the next one, because each time you hit a milestone, it's like a reward.

You may think these numbers are astronomical or unattainable, but I have seen my students go through the same limiting beliefs, thinking *This is too hard* or *I can't do it*, only to turn everything around and accomplish incredible things when they begin to ask, "How can I?" instead. These numbers are also likely not as much as you think they are, because we are talking bare-bones expenses. In the event of an emergency, such as job loss, you're not going out for dinner, you're not getting your nails done—you are only paying for the things you must absolutely pay for to keep living and not default on payments, like your rent or mortgage and your car.

Saving your catch-all emergency fund is the way you are going to ensure your future financial success because it is going to be the cushion that saves you from digging yourself into a bigger hole when an unexpected event happens because they always happen, and if you fail to plan, plan to fail.

An emergency fund is also integral in helping you pay off your debt. While this may seem counterintuitive—why would I put money into an emergency fund instead of my debt?—your emergency fund will prevent you from going further into debt. When you don't have an emergency fund, typically what happens is that you exhaust all your funds paying off your debt, then you have no money left over for when life happens. This results in going into debt while trying to dig yourself out of debt that is the result of not planning in the first place. It becomes a vicious cycle that's difficult to break out of—the way to interrupt that pattern is to build that "oh shit fund" and keep it available for when things inevitably go south (because that's life). Your emergency fund is your safeguard. It is a necessity, not a luxury.

If you have debt and you're reading this, I want you to save your first baby emergency fund of $1,000. Then, start dividing your savings up between your emergency fund and your debt (and other goals) simultaneously. You're allowed to work on more than one goal at once.

RULE SIX: PUT YOUR MONEY WHERE IT WILL WORK THE HARDEST FOR YOU

My students always ask, "Nicole, I have X dollars and some debt, but I'd also like to start growing this money through investing (because it's sexy). Where should I put it?" The mathematical answer is to put your money where it will work the hardest for you. Unsure where your money will work the hardest for you? It works the hardest wherever it earns or saves you the highest interest.

Let's look at an example to illustrate:

- Sally has a thousand dollars but is not sure what to do with it.

- Sally has a credit card balance of a thousand dollars, and she is being charged 24.99 percent interest on the balance.

- Sally also wants to start investing and growing her money, so she is thinking about putting it into the stock market. A safe assumption for a return in the stock market could be around 7 percent.

Where will Sally's money work hardest? The 24.99 percent interest debt or the 7 percent potential gain in the stock market?

Undoubtedly, Sally's money will work the hardest with the 24.99 percent interest on her debt. This number is a lot higher than her potential return in the stock market (that is, what she could make). By paying off her debt, she is automatically getting a 24.99 percent return on her money instead of a potential 7 percent in the stock market.

A good rule of thumb to follow is to focus on paying off any debts with over 5 percent interest, and anything under that could potentially wait (as long as you are still making the minimum payments at least). An example of when it might not make sense to pay off your debt is with a mortgage, which could have lower interest rates of 2–3 percent.

Imagine this alternative example:

- Sally has $200,000.

- Sally has a $200,000 mortgage at 2.5 percent, but she'd also like to invest the money.

If Sally pays off the mortgage, that $200,000 is gone forever and Sally owns a paid-off home. However, if Sally invests that $200,000, gaining a 7 percent annual return, theoretically she could earn a $14,000 profit in year one. Based on this example, Sally could use the profit from the investment to pay the monthly mortgage, and in twenty-five years, when the house is paid off, Sally will still have the $200,000 and a paid-off home. Alternatively, if Sally took the $200,000 and invested it, earning an average 7 percent annually, in the stock market and continued to make the mortgage payments herself over the next twenty-five years, that $200,000 could have grown to over $1,085,000 (a.k.a. $885,000 in *free* money) just by putting her money in the right places.

That said, what makes sense from a math and numbers standpoint may not always feel good to you personally. This is why personal finance is *personal*. This is an exception to the rule: even though it may make more sense to invest the money instead of paying off Sally's mortgage, if Sally feels better about having a paid-off mortgage and is okay with forgoing the potential returns and growth, then that's okay too. It's all about what works best for you personally in your own life.

RULE SEVEN: WHY PAY MORE (WPM PRINCIPLE)

Finally, we have the WPM Principle: *Why Pay More*. I came up with this principle after spending time working in the head office of one of Canada's largest retailers (my first job right out of university). I joined a management training program, which had me rotating through various departments in the company, so I could gain a holistic view of how it operated.

One of the departments I worked in was product development. To be honest, I was super psyched about that rotation. I was so excited to be able to assist on plans and strategies to innovate and bring cool new products to market. What I eventually discovered was that this department worked much differently than I expected. Instead of an emphasis on innovation, there seemed to be an emphasis on copying—copying other products and slapping a new label on them, to be more exact. What I learned is that many of the private-label products you see in stores are carbon copies of the name-brand version, just at a discounted price. In many instances, they are literally the exact same product, made with the same ingredients, the same parts, the same processes, and in the same factories as the name-brand ones. I found out this is done across many industries, including grocery, pharmaceuticals, and fashion. What happens in many instances is that manufacturing plants have a certain capacity to create products, and creating X number of products could be the same cost to the plant as creating y number of products, so these manufacturers will work with multiple companies, create a single product, and just put different labels or tags on it. There could be two products that are the same, but selling for astronomically different prices. What I found was that the price we pay isn't necessarily set based on the cost of the product, but based on the marketing and consumer perception of the product.

It was at this point that I realized buying name-brand for many things was a scam. We pay more for nothing more than better marketing. Essentially, their advertisers did a better job at convincing us this product is the one we wanted, for whatever reason, even though it could be the same as the one sitting beside it for half the price. It was then that I determined it made no sense to me to pay more for something, if I could get the same benefit (or value) for less. Thus, the WPM Principle was born—because seriously, *Why Pay More?*

I've continued this concept throughout my life in many areas, and I even used it when I decided what car I was going to buy. I initially wanted the expensive luxury SUV when I bought my last car, but I died a little inside when I saw the monthly payment. I went over to another cheaper dealership and found an SUV that looked almost exactly the same (save for the logo on the back) and had the moon roof, heated seats, and GPS system I wanted, but it was a fraction of the cost. Why would I pay two to three times more simply for a label, when the cheaper version had everything I wanted? I promise you—this concept has changed my life in so many ways and put so much money back into my pockets without me having to give up things I love or change my lifestyle at all. I'm still getting the same benefit. I'm just paying less for it. You can also bring this principle into your daily financial decisions when comparing the amount of happiness you derive from a purchase to how much you're actually paying for it. A lot of us equate spending more money with being more wealthy and more successful—by spending more, we are showing our "best selves" to the world. But what if spending more was simply just *spending more?* Remember: You don't build wealth by spending all of it.

- Why pay more than you *have* to for the things you buy?

- Why pay more than you *want* to for the stuff you're getting?

- Why pay more than you *need* to for a level of fulfillment and happiness that works for *you* personally?

So many of us get caught up in paying more simply because we believe we should, because everyone does it, because it's expected of us, or because it's the norm—but remember what I said about doing what the average person does? It gets you average lifetime results, and the average person isn't happy or wealthy.

Question your motivations to get to the root cause before you decide to spend. Ask yourself: *How much do I need to spend to reach my peak level of happiness? Does spending more actually bring me more true happiness?* Remember, we're looking for a feeling of satisfaction, not overconsumption.

Ask yourself:

- Is spending an extra $10,000 on imported floral arrangements for my wedding going to make me *that* much happier?

- How long will I have to work to earn that money? Will I get more happiness spending it elsewhere?

- Is paying an extra six hundred dollars a month for a "luxury" car going to bring me more fulfillment and joy, or would I rather have that extra money to put toward that vacation I've always wanted to go on?

- Is getting this sweater on credit going to make me feel better about myself, or am I just going to throw it in the back of my closet and spend the next ten years making the minimum payment?

- Do I want to have to work overtime to pay back the debt, or would I rather spend that time doing something I truly enjoy instead?

CHAPTER 6

ARE YOU **ASKING** **BROKE** QUESTIONS?

I used to spend what felt like hours in the toilet paper aisle of the grocery store, trying to find the best deal. I'd sift through the double and triple rolls and bonus packs, in a store that didn't have their stuff properly labeled, all in the name of potentially saving a few bucks (hopefully). The decision of what pack of toilet paper I should buy became daunting and, if I'm truthful, kind of stressful. I felt like I had no idea what I was doing, that I was making the wrong decision and throwing money away by potentially selecting the wrong pack. I'd go back and forth between brands that seemed almost identical, trying to compute the number of toilet paper squares I was getting for my money—because that's what being good with money is about, isn't it? That's how I was going to change my financial situation—by getting the best deal on toilet paper, right? Wrong.

I grew up believing the things that impact your financial situation are those small transactions, like buying coffee in the morning and not overspending on toilet paper. In reality, budgeting and couponing will never make you rich. They'll never help you build real wealth. Simply put, they will have you focusing on the wrong things. I was stuck in that broke mindset, spending an embarrassing amount of time focusing on broke questions like, "Which toilet paper is the better buy?" and constantly focusing on the small details that, in the end, really had no meaningful impact on my financial situation.

So many of us are preoccupied with asking broke questions, putting our energy and focus into things that just take time away from the big things that make a difference. Many of us are so focused on broke questions, it's keeping us stuck. We get so caught up in looking at all the little details and the little ways we can *save more*, that we forget the *big things*. Instead of asking broke questions, we need to start focusing on the wealthy mindset questions.

Asking broke questions consists of:

- Spending ten minutes in the toilet paper aisle trying to figure out which price is the best deal

- Spending hours or days comparing high-interest savings accounts because one has a 0.3 percent difference (which is literally pennies)

- Wondering if buying a coffee in the morning is the reason you're stuck financially, instead of looking at the big things (like your house, car, and consumer debt)

- Looking at two investment options or accounts that are essentially the same, but being paralyzed and unable to choose

Broke questions are a problem for three main reasons:

1. They are based on a belief that our small habits influence all the results we have in our lives.

2. When we ask broke questions, we end up putting ourselves into analysis paralysis, which is when we get so stuck in analyzing the minute details, we become unable to make a choice.

3. Asking broke questions prevents us from asking the right questions that have the real ability to change our financial situation (i.e., wealthy mindset questions).

Asking broke questions causes **analysis paralysis**, which stops us from taking action. Instead of getting things done, moving forward, and seeing results, we get caught up in getting more information and thinking we're *not able* to move forward because we don't know enough. When it comes to personal finance or money-related decisions, this manifests itself as us believing all this finance shit is too hard. So we don't take action. We give up. Asking broke questions becomes a precursor to self-sabotage (getting in your own damn way).

"It's too confusing."

"There are too many options."

"It's too hard."

We get stuck being broke because we are stuck asking broke questions, not realizing that *some* movement in the right direction is better than no movement at all. How many times have you believed taking action required an all-or-nothing approach? You either did it all the way, or you didn't do it at all. When was the last time you said to yourself, "OMG I'd love to work out, I'd love to read, I'd love to clean my house and reorganize that room, [insert your "wishful to-do" here], but I don't have the time"? One of the reasons you likely believe you don't have the time is because you're taking an all-or-nothing approach. (The other is that procrastination can actually be a form of self-sabotage, but that's a whole other lesson entirely.) You're stuck believing that you must go all in or not in at all. Lucky for you, there's a little secret: Everything in life isn't black or white. It's not all or nothing—there are shades of gray—and small steps in the right direction are *still* steps in the right direction. We can apply this to our finances as well—why wait until things are 100 percent perfect to get started? Getting out there and getting the quick, small wins can psychologically push us further and harder.

If you want to work out, why not start by working out ten minutes a day? Or one day a week? Why does it have to be a five-day commitment? The simple answer: It doesn't. That's just the rule you've made up in your mind about it. If you want to read more, how about starting with five minutes a day before you go to bed? If you want to organize your room, why not start with just the closet, or just fifteen minutes each day? We forget that we have options to start getting closer to our goals. Because isn't ten minutes a day or one day a week better than nothing? Can't save a thousand dollars? Save a hundred. Can't save a hundred dollars? Save ten. Starting somewhere is still starting, and no one ever changed their life by staying where they are. Commit to making the change and take some action steps toward your goals each day—no matter how "small" they are. So many of us choose to do nothing because we're stuck in analysis paralysis, stuck in an "all or nothing" attitude, and stuck asking broke questions. But the wealthy mindset questions? Those are the questions that can change your life.

Is the reason you're not a millionaire right now because you bought the wrong toilet paper? No. So why is it the focus of your financial journey? Where you spend your money is irrelevant, as long as you are spending it on things that truly bring you joy and happiness. As long as you are following the money rules we talked about in chapter 5, you can spend your money as you please.

Do our bad habits add up to money wasted over time? Yes, but only if they're "bad habits." Money is only wasted if you've spent it on things that don't reflect your values, like spending based on societal expectations, a perceived void, to fit in, or to be liked or wanted. Money spent on things that bring you true happiness is never a waste, even if it is your morning

Starbucks, and even if it means you could have had $70,000 in the bank in ten years in place of morning coffee if you invested your daily Starbucks money into the markets instead. On the other hand, if you continue to buy shit you don't need, then you can't get angry when you aren't reaching your goals or when you aren't achieving the things that truly matter and contribute to the overall satisfaction in your life. As long as you understand the tradeoffs, your priorities, what brings you true happiness, and you act accordingly, then the small things—the broke questions—don't matter. If you've decided you *love* Starbucks in the morning and having it makes you happy, instead of trying to restrict yourself (like budgets do with their emphasis on scarcity and lack), focus on cutting the shit you don't love.

Do you love electronics? No? Then maybe you don't get the newest and best phone when it comes out because that's not a value to you. Are you happy bringing your lunch to work? Yes? Great, that's money saved from not spending on shit you don't care about. Now you can guiltlessly put it toward stuff you do love (like your Starbucks). Ultimately, it's about what is most important to you, and what feels like enough and not more. Cut the excess, like the shit that sits in the back of your closet or gets charged to your account monthly but goes unused. When we stop focusing on broke questions and begin to focus on the wealthy mindset ones, we can change our lives without feeling restricted.

WEALTHY MINDSET QUESTIONS

Okay, Nicole, I'll stop focusing my energy on broke questions, since they're preventing me from seeing real success with my money. I'll redirect my attention to asking wealthy mindset questions. What exactly is a wealthy mindset question?

Simply put: A **wealthy mindset question** asks you about your financial situation from a wealthy mindset point of view. They're questions about the things and situations in your life that can make substantial change in your financial situation.

Nine Wealthy Mindset Questions:

1. How much should I save? (*Not,* Should I save?)

2. How much should I invest? (*Not,* Should I invest?)

3. How much should I spend when buying a house?

4. Should I buy or should I rent?

5. Should I go into debt for my wedding?

6. Should I buy a high-end vehicle on financing?

7. Should I spend money via my credit cards when I don't have the cash?

8. Should I pay down my student loans faster?

9. How much should I be saving for retirement?

Asking wealthy mindset questions stops you from focusing on the few-dollars-and-cents price differential between two packages of toilet paper and prompts you to look at the bigger-picture items that can truly move the needle for you financially. These situations are the ones that have the possibility to truly propel you forward in life—or, if you're not cognizant of them, to hold you back.

There are some common themes I've seen with my students in terms of life events that can either make or break you, so I'm going to get into each one of them here to teach you what to look out for and how you can plan to move closer to adopting a wealthy mindset with each one of these questions.

HOW MUCH SHOULD I SAVE? (NOT, SHOULD I SAVE?)

Stop asking if you should save or invest. The answer is always yes! Yes, you should be saving and investing. Saving is not depriving yourself. It's making your future self a priority. It's making your future goals and dreams a priority. When you can get to a point where you no longer see saving for your future goals as deprivation but as living true to your values, that's when you'll start to see real change.

Financial experts like to tell you that you should be saving a percentage of your paycheck, but I think those ambiguous percentages restrict us rather than help us. Those percentages are for the average person, and we're not trying to be average with our money. Remember: The average person is in debt, unhappy, and working a job they hate, yet unsure if they'll ever "get to stop working." To get something different, we have to do something different, and that's why you're here. You don't want to be average, so we must make different choices than the average person would. It's all going to come down to understanding your expenses, bringing awareness to your spending (instead of wondering where your money has gone), and understanding how much of your life you had to trade for the shit you bought.

It comes down to your goals. It comes down to a tradeoff. Would you rather keep throwing money away on shit you push to the back of your closet, or would you rather buy that house, have a wedding, stop working so much, travel more, or become financially independent? Your choice. To know how much you should be saving, you need to get a clear understanding of your goals. Simply telling me you want to be rich is not enough.

HOW DO I DETERMINE HOW MUCH
I SHOULD BE SAVING?

1. **Calculate your savings goal(s).** What *exactly* do you want? Describe it in so much detail there is no mistaking what you're going after or what you will need to do to get there. I recommend using the SMART goal method to write out your goals. (Yup, we're taking it back to high school with this one!) Each of the letters in SMART goal represent a word that describes its individual component of the goal:

   Specific: providing enough details so there is no confusion on what needs to be done and when.

   Measurable: including timelines, deadlines, and specifics that can assist in measuring success toward the goal.

   Attainable: something that has been done, or can be done, based on your life circumstances.

   Realistic: it's something that fits in with our overall life plan, and doesn't put unrealistic expectations on the achievement of the goal.

   Time-bound: a timeline, a start date, and an end date.

   Turning your goal into a SMART goal is imperative in being able to achieve it. Too many people have wishy-washy goals, like *I want to save money*, or *I want to buy a house*, but they feel paralyzed about what they need to do specifically to get there. You can't create a plan when you don't even know what you really want. How much money do you want to save? Why? For what? By when? Is that timeline realistic? Have you reviewed the numbers to see if it works?

Setting a rather vague goal that says, "I want to save more money" and setting a SMART goal that says, "I am going to save $15,000 in twenty-four months from tomorrow's date for a down payment on a $300,000 house" are completely different and will result in completely different results.

The goal is specific, because it tells you exactly what will be done and when.

It's measurable because we have specific numbers ($15,000 in twenty-four months).

Attainable because we've worked out the numbers based on our own personal financial situation, and we know we have the resources to make it happen.

It's realistic because we've done the homework to make sure it's not only attainable, but fits in with our overall life plan.

And it's time-bound, because we've given ourselves the date for completion.

2. **Do the math.** Once your SMART savings goal is complete, you are going to reverse-engineer it to see exactly what you need to do today to achieve your goal of the future. (I prefer to break my goals down monthly, but you can also do biweekly to make things easier, if that aligns better with your pay schedule.)

   Divide your total goal amount by the number of savings periods (weeks, months, etc.) from now until you plan to achieve your goal.

Example: If I want to save $15,000 in twenty-four months, I will need to save $625 a month ($15,000 divided by 24).

3. **Adjust your goal as needed.** Once you've determined what you need to save on a per-pay-period basis, then you can review it. Does this number feel good to you? Can you save more? Is it a bit too high? If you can save more, that means you can achieve your goal in a shorter amount of time, or put that money toward other goals to work on simultaneously.

   Don't be afraid to extend your timeline out further if you need more time to save. Adjust it until you establish a savings amount and timeline that feels good to you. It's important for your SMART goal to be attainable and realistic.

HOW MUCH SHOULD I INVEST? (*NOT*, SHOULD I INVEST?)

Investing is not a "should I" question. It's both a "how much *can* I contribute" and a "what are my overall financial goals" question.

- You will never save your way to retirement.

- You will never save your way to financial independence.

- You will never save your way to a feeling of safety and security in the long term.

This is because your savings count on you trading hours of your life for money—this is known as your active income—and when we only ever trade hours for dollars, there will always be a limit to what we can make.

For you in your profession, there's a limit to how much someone will pay you to do your job. There's also a limit to the number of hours there are in a day.

The key is to be able to earn money while you sleep (i.e., have your money making you *more* money, without you physically having to work for it). This is where investing comes in: Investing is a necessary step to being able to have enough money to retire, and reach any semblance of financial independence.

Additionally, when you only trade time for money, your lifestyle is entirely dependent on you getting up and working. Having a job may give you a feeling of perceived safety, but even the best companies downsize, make roles redundant, restructure, and have layoffs. Real safety and security with your finances comes from the ability to receive income or money from sources other than just your nine-to-five.

Frankly, even if we are focusing on just saving our money, it means we are losing money—we can thank our little friend inflation for that (more on this in chapter 8).

Unfortunately, too many people don't save or invest—why? Because there's a disconnect between their actions today and the benefit in the future. Many people can imagine their lives in five years, or maybe even ten...but can you imagine your life in forty years? Have you ever thought about the details of your day-to-day when you're seventy years old? For most people, I'm going to say probably not.

But pretending we aren't going to get there, and turning a blind eye to our inevitable futures, leaves us at risk for financial and economic instability.

And if you're someone with the false belief that Social Security will take care of you in old age, then here's a scary statistic for you: Individuals who exist on Social Security benefits alone don't live far above the poverty line, which is roughly $1,132 a month for a single person in 2022.[46]

HOW TO DETERMINE HOW MUCH
TO SAVE AND INVEST

So this raises the question: How do you determine how much money you need to save and invest to reach your goals?

The simple answer is to determine the parameters for your goal: how much money you need in total, and when you need it by. Then you can use a compound interest calculator to help you work backward to figure out what you need to save today (you can find one of these online with a simple search).

For example, if you wanted to have a $10,000 investment account grown in ten years, with an average rate of return of 7 percent (this will change depending on what you're investing in), you'd need to save (and then invest) approximately sixty dollars per month to make this happen.

When we're talking about investing for retirement, the rules get a little more complicated.

The standard advice for retirement saving is that you should be saving 10 percent of your annual income, and investing it, for retirement. However, I believe the lack of specificity in this rule will prove to be detrimental for many people—it's a good starting point to get some sort of an idea what your numbers *could* look like, but is by no means an accurate representation of what every single person should be saving and investing.

---

46   investopedia.com/articles/personal-finance/022516/what-will-social-security-look-when-you-retire.asp

Let's look at an example of two people (Sally and Fred) who are saving and investing 10 percent of their annual $60,000 income ($6,000 annually, or $500 a month), and what it actually means for them in real terms.

SCENARIO BREAKDOWN

Sally and Fred decide they are going to follow traditional advice, and start putting five hundred dollars a month into investments for their retirement. They start doing this at age twenty-five and plan to continue until the standard retirement age of sixty-five, so they have forty years for their money to work for them.

At an average return of 7 percent, Sally and Fred would each have $1,235,771 in their account when they were ready to retire. Based on the 4 percent rule, which says you can safely withdraw 4 percent of your stock market investments a year in retirement without risk of running out of money, Sally and Fred would each be able to take out roughly $49,000 annually to live on.[47]

Sounds like a hefty sum, right? Let's take a look at how this could play out for each of them based on their unique lifestyle choices and needs.

Scenario One: Sally

Sally and her partner Phil decide to retire at the age of sixty-five. Sally had her personal retirement savings providing her with $49,000 annually, and Phil had a pension that gave him another $50,000 a year. Combined they had a retirement income of almost $100,000 per year.

Sally and Phil had always dreamed of selling their big-city home in Upstate New York and downsizing to a small trailer in Florida to soak up the sun in retirement. After paying off any outstanding mortgages on

_____

47   www.investopedia.com/terms/f/four-percent-rule.asp

the property, and the purchase of their new trailer, this left Sally and Phil with over $300,000 in cash that they could also use to fund their lifestyle.

They weren't big spenders, preferring to take up low-cost activities in their leisure, like camping, hiking, and going to the beach. After running their expenses, they realized that they actually only need $75,000 a year to maintain their current lifestyle.

This means that Sally theoretically could have saved less money each month throughout the forty years of investing, giving her more money to spend on things she needed, wanted, or enjoyed in her earlier years. Instead of saving $1,200,000, she would have only needed to build an account of about half that to give her the life she wanted—meaning she did not need to save and invest 10 percent of her income.

Scenario Two: Fred

Fred's situation was a bit different—his partner, Anya, had no pension or retirement savings of her own, meaning the couple would have approximately $49,000 between the two of them to live on.

Their children lived nearby, so they had no intention of selling their home and moving to a less expensive area, even though they still had a mortgage on the property.

For leisure, Fred and Anya enjoyed traveling, and planned to do more of it once they had more time available after they left their jobs.

Between their fixed expenses (i.e., things you cannot easily change, like your mortgage), and their travel and other leisure expenses, Fred and Anya realized they would be spending roughly $85,000 annually—putting them over the safe withdrawal rate of 4 percent. This puts the couple at risk of running out of money, and potentially needing to continue working (at least part-time) to supplement their income.

Instead of building a bank account of $1,200,000 for retirement, the couple really needed to save $2,125,000 to fund the kind of life they wanted. Fred would have needed to increase his contribution to his retirement savings by $350 a month to provide them with the ability to live their desired lifestyle (a total of $850 a month). This means Fred would have needed to save more than 10 percent of his income.

This is why I don't like using blanket percentages as the rule for how much you "should be" saving or investing, as it doesn't look at the individual person. Personal finance is personal—you can use a rule to help you get started, but you should always be working out your own numbers and goals to get the specifics you need to ensure you can hit your goals. The worst thing to me would be spending forty years working toward a goal, only to find out I didn't do things I could have done (because I saved more than I needed to), or I didn't save enough. There's no going back in time and rewriting our lives.

Other Considerations

There are so many other factors that could influence the viability of their plans, such as:

- The mix of their investments (different investments provide different returns, meaning where you put your money can influence just how much money you actually make)
- The timeline for investing (the longer you have before you need the money, the harder your money and compound interest can work for you)
    › Starting your investing journey earlier, or ending it earlier (in the case of early retirement) can drastically impact how much money you make

- The expenses and fees on their investments (these compound against you and eat into the growth of your money—and even something as simple as a 1 percent difference in fees could cost you $590,000 in retirement savings)[48]

- The accounts used for investing (if you didn't use an account with tax benefits, you could be hit with a hefty bill once you start to withdraw)

THE 4 PERCENT RULE

The 4 percent rule for retirement is a practical rule of thumb that may be used by retirees to decide how much they should withdraw from their retirement funds each year.

The purpose of this rule is to provide a guideline on how much of your investments you can withdraw annually to create a stream of income, while maintaining a balance (that will continue growing and working for you) that you can use in the future to continue funding your lifestyle. The goal is to have your money generate more money through the powers of investing and compound interest—essentially, you trade places with your money: you get to relax, and your money goes to work.[49]

A quick way to calculate how much money you need to retire on, using the 4 percent rule, is to take your annual spend (how much money you need to sustain the lifestyle you desire) and multiply it by twenty-five.

For example, if you spend $40,000 per year, you would need to have $1,000,000 invested to provide you with the ability to withdraw 4 percent annually.

---

48 nerdwallet.com/blog/investing/millennial-retirement-fees-one-percent-half-million-savings-impact/

49 nvestopedia.com/terms/f/four-percent-rule.asp

$1,000,000 / 4 percent

There are some criticisms of the rule, which say 4 percent is actually too much (they recommend a 3 percent withdrawal instead), or that you can actually spend more than 4 percent (allowing you to spend 5 percent annually instead).[50, 51]

It's easy to see that investing is not a "should I" (broke) question, it's a "how much should I contribute to reach my financial goals and find security long-term" question—and the earlier you start, the easier it is, and the more your money can work *for you* (that's the dream, isn't it?).

HOW MUCH SHOULD I SPEND WHEN BUYING A HOUSE?

Many people buy houses outside their means because "the bank told them they could" without thinking about the impact of signing onto a twenty-five-year loan and what it means for their life. Unfortunately, I've seen this time and time again, where emotions take over, rationality goes out the window, and people fail to work out how much money they should be spending based on the lifestyle they want to live.

Buying an expensive house is okay when you understand the tradeoff costs (maybe it means you can't travel, you must eat all your meals at home, and you have to look for low-cost entertainment), and you're living on less than you make, paying your future self first, and investing early and often. If you decide an expensive house is more important to you than, say, having a car, then that's okay because there is always a tradeoff when we make a finite amount of money. The key here is to make sure it's more important to you

---

50   marketwatch.com/story/whats-the-problem-with-the-4-rule-11596799147

51   seekingalpha.com/article/1228791-is-the-4-percent-rule-becoming-the-3-percent-rule

personally, and you're not doing it to create a certain appearance, because you think you have to, or because you haven't run your numbers on what feels good to *you* (not what the bank told you that you can afford). The bank doesn't know *you*. They know their risk and a formula that looks at how much income and debt you have, but they don't know your personal lifestyle. They don't know what your hopes and dreams are. They don't know if you plan to have three kids and will need to pay for them all to go to daycare at the same time.

People buy expensive houses and then a lot of them go broke, hence the term "house poor," which is used to describe people who have no money left over for life after buying their house. Overspending on your home can prevent you from being able to save and invest. Unfortunately, what I've seen many times is that, instead of changing their lifestyle in other ways to make up for spending more on their home, many continue to spend as they did before they bought the expensive home, filling the gap with credit, digging themselves deeper and deeper into a hole with consumer debt. Keeping up appearances and keeping up with the Joneses.

Another big mistake that I see people make is buying the wrong property at the wrong time. For example, buying a studio condo when they're thinking about having kids next year (have you thought about where you're going to put the kid?), or buying a home in an area they don't want to live in or that isn't feasible for their personal situation. They put themselves in situations where they *have* to sell, which is the biggest mistake you can make. Whenever you buy a house or invest, and you put yourself in a situation where you *have* to sell, that's when you can lose money. We never want to be in a position where we *have* to sell. We want to be able to *choose* to sell when it makes the most sense for us personally and financially. This takes some planning on the back end, which again, many people unfortunately do not do.

You need to be buying a home that will suit your needs for the long term, meaning over five years. People forget that, in addition to the cost of the home, it's also expensive to buy and sell. Commissions, fees, taxes, they all add up—quickly. Buying for the long term doesn't necessarily mean buying a huge house. It simply means buying a house that suits your lifestyle. One you can *choose* to sell, but that you won't be in a situation where you *have* to sell. Like stock markets, real estate markets also fluctuate in value (although not as quickly or as often as stocks). If you *have* to sell and the markets suck, guess what, you're probably losing money. And don't kid yourself by thinking that if you live in an area with rising housing prices, you'll always make money when you sell. That's not the case, and I've seen too many people fall into this trap and be out tens to hundreds of thousands of dollars. No, that's not a typo.

A good rule of thumb is to look at what the bank has told you you can spend, and reduce this amount by 10 percent. Do you have to do this? No, but if you can, the savings can be huge. Imagine you got approved for a $400,000 mortgage, but instead of spending $400,000 you spent $360,000 (10 percent less) with a 2.25 percent interest rate (the higher your interest rate, the higher your payments would be, and the more you would pay in interest). Let's also say you have $40,000 to put down for the down payment (roughly 10 percent). If you spent $360,000, your monthly mortgage payments would be $1,376 per month. You would pay a total of $98,000 in interest over a twenty-five-year term. If you spent the full $400,000, your mortgage monthly would be $1,548. You would pay a total of $110,000 in interest. This does not include any mortgage insurance for less than 20 percent down (i.e., CMHC or PMI).

If you spent 10 percent less, this would mean an additional $172 roughly in your pocket every month. If we invested this amount, earning an average of 8 percent interest, adjusted for inflation, you would have over $150,000 *plus* your paid-off house that would likely be worth more than you paid for it (in the long term, housing markets on average have gone up). Leave that $150,000 invested and never contribute another penny, and in another twenty-five years you would have over a million dollars.

Small changes in our big expenses can be the difference between becoming wealthy or being house poor. The best way to protect yourself when buying a house is by buying defensively. Remember when you took drivers' ed, and the first thing they taught you was that you can't control what anyone else on the road is doing, but you can control yourself? Apply that same principle to buying a house. You can't control what the markets will do, but you can control your actions—and your actions are the single best predictor of how successful you will be.

TO BUY YOUR HOUSE DEFENSIVELY, ASK YOURSELF THREE QUESTIONS:

DO I HAVE AT LEAST 10 PERCENT SAVED UP?

You typically want to have 5 percent saved for the down payment at minimum and depending on your area, you will want another 2.5 percent for closing costs and 2.5 percent as a cushion (these numbers will vary based on your location, so check with a local realtor or mortgage broker to confirm). The last thing you ever want to do is spend your last dollar buying a home. Something will *always* come up, so be prepared. Start to plan, and expect the unexpected.

CAN I STAY IN THE HOME FOR AT LEAST FIVE YEARS?

Stop trying to buy a home for the short term and focus on the long term. Markets always go up and down, but the only time you lose money is when you *have* to sell. Otherwise, it's a paper loss. This doesn't mean you can't sell your home in less time if the numbers make sense, but you should never put yourself in a situation where you *have* to sell in the short term (I'm looking at you, people who are buying one-bedroom condos and expecting to have multiple kids in the next few years).

Pro Tip: If you can afford it, it might make sense to buy your second home first. Buying and selling is expensive, but if you can get into a home that will suit your needs for the long term (over ten years), you could save tens of thousands over your lifetime (which could be hundreds of thousands if invested properly). This doesn't mean you should overspend on your home, but if you have the option of spending slightly more and getting a home that suits your needs longer, it could be a great way to save a ton of money.

DO I SEE ANY MAJOR LIFE CHANGES COMING UP IN THE SHORT TERM?

Are you going back to school? Having kids? Taking a sabbatical? If you are planning on doing something that could decrease your income or lead to a highly volatile job (meaning you don't know how secure your employment is), this *needs* to be taken into consideration if you're thinking of buying a home. This doesn't necessarily mean you *can't* buy a home, but it does mean you should spend less than what the bank is offering you, or look at alternative ways to provide for extra income when your income is lowered, such as buying a home with an in-law apartment and renting it out, if and when needed, to bring in some more money without changing your lifestyle (this is called house-hacking, and it is one of the best ways to bring the costs of your home down so you can put your money elsewhere).

SHOULD I BUY OR RENT?

Ah, the age-old debate. There really is no right or wrong answer here, as the specifics are entirely personal. Yet, there are so many shades of gray.

Here are some of the main viewpoints in favor of buying a home:

- Eventually, the home's paid off and you have no monthly payments (aside from taxes and upkeep).

- Home ownership is a forced savings plan.

- Home ownership provides a sense of security.

- The value of homes tends to go up over time (not by just your down payment amount, but by the full value of the home).

- You can house-hack and reduce your costs (or live for free).

- You may get tax credits for the interest you pay on your mortgage (in some countries).

Here are some of the main viewpoints in favor of renting:

- You're not tied down to one area.

- You're not responsible for the upkeep and maintenance costs.

- Renting isn't throwing your money away because you get a place to live.

- Instead of using your money for a down payment, you can put it into the markets and invest it.

Now, I do see the points for renting, and some people may feel it's the better decision for them. Maybe they live in a very expensive area, and buying a home just isn't possible. Maybe they move around a lot for work. Maybe they would rather not have the worry and responsibility of owning a home. However, from a financial standpoint, I personally believe buying is better for most people. But again, personal finance is personal, so do what works best for your life.

PROS OF BUYING A HOME

- **Eventually, the house is paid off and you have no monthly payments (aside from taxes and upkeep).**

  In twenty-five years (or fifteen or thirty, depending on your mortgage term), you'll have no payments to make for your home again. That means that, if you bought a home at twenty-five, by fifty you could be living for free, essentially. When you rent, you will always have a payment.

- **Owning a home is a forced savings plan.**

  Most people mean well—meaning they know they should be saving, but they don't. A home is a forced savings plan. Sure, you are paying interest on the loan—but when you rent, you're also paying a similar amount of money every month, except in the end you're no further ahead.

- **Homeownership provides a sense of security.**

  When you rent, you have no control over rental increases. In some cases, you can face eviction even if you're the perfect tenant (for example, if the owner or a member of their family wants to move in). When you own your home, it is yours, and no one is ever going to kick you out.

- **Homes tend to go up in value (not just by your down payment amount, but by the full value of the home).**

  Very few people buy their home with cash, which means most finance a portion (in the form of a mortgage). When the value of the home increases, it goes up by the total cost of the home, not what you personally put into it.

  At the very least, the value of the home will go up with inflation (about 2 percent a year), or it could increase by 10 percent a year. This means you're making 2–10 percent every year on hundreds of thousands of dollars of the bank's money (this is called using leverage, or other people's money, to build wealth).

- **You can house-hack and reduce your living costs (or live completely for free).**
  If you buy a home with a separate suite (like a basement apartment), you can rent it out. In some cases, you may even make enough money to cover your mortgage.

- **You may get tax credits for the interest you pay on your mortgage (in some countries).**
  At the time of writing, in the US you can claim interest payments on your mortgage on your taxes, which means you will pay less in taxes. (Hello to savings just for owning your home!)

RENTING

I could make an argument for many of these points from the renting camp because, although in my experience it makes more sense for most people to buy a home, the reality is that everyone's situation is different, and personal finance is personal.

If you're someone who moves around a lot, or lives in an expensive area where you couldn't comfortably afford to buy, then renting can make more sense for you. If you're not sure where you want to live long-term and don't know if you'll still want to live in the same location in the short term, then renting might be a better option than buying and *having* to sell. If you see major changes coming to your income in the short term, if you haven't saved up the down payment plus cushion, then renting could be a good option for you personally.

Remember: Buying and selling homes is expensive, so it's likely not something you want to do all the time. Additionally, buying and selling in a short period of time is speculative because you don't know with any certainty what will happen in the short term, so this sort of buying/investing is generally something I would discourage.

Additionally, I believe that, if you can rent for less than the unrecoverable costs of homeownership, and you invest the difference, technically you could come out ahead. The unrecoverable costs to homeownership are all the expenses that come along with owning a home that you don't usually get back—expenses like property taxes, home insurance, maintenance, and your mortgage interest. If you totaled up the average cost of those things for a home in your area and could rent for less than those costs and then invested the difference in your savings, then mathematically you could come out ahead.

The problem with this is that it's generally hard to find a property to rent that fits these criteria, and the average person would likely not save or invest the difference. But you're not the average person, remember? So make sure you're gathering all the information and making an educated and informed decision that helps you live in alignment with your values and goals while remembering the tradeoff costs.

PROS OF RENTING

- **You're not tied down to one area.**
  If you are someone who moves frequently, buying a home is likely not in your best interest. The costs of buying and selling would likely eat into any profits you made from the price appreciation of owning.

- **You're not responsible for the upkeep and maintenance costs.**
  Depending on where you live, upkeep and maintenance costs are likely worked into the price of the rent. However, that's not a hard and fast rule. There are some areas where landlords are actively

losing money every month when all expenses are considered. No, not all landlords make tons of money, and some pay out of their own pocket every month for the property they rent out because there is a shortfall in what they collect versus what they pay. These landlords are typically hoping the property goes up in value to make up for the monthly losses. (This is highly speculative, a.k.a. gambling, and not something I would ever recommend; however, people do it all the time.)

- **Renting isn't throwing your money away because you get a place to live.**
  Yes, it's true. Renting could be seen as a service because you are getting a place to live in exchange for your money. It's important to understand the tradeoff cost of paying rent versus paying that money into a mortgage and making sure you're happy with the outcome.

- **Instead of using your money for a down payment, you can put it into the markets and invest it.**
  While this is possible, there are two things are wrong with this:

  1. The majority of people won't do that.

  2. You're making a return on your down payment only, as opposed to making a return on the total price of the home (meaning you're investing $50,000 instead of $500,000 of which $450,000 was someone else's money).

LIVING IN AN EXPENSIVE AREA

So you're listening to this advice thinking, *Shit, I live in a super expensive area. No one can afford to buy here. I can barely afford rent.*

Does this mean you can't get out ahead? No.

One of two things may need to happen:

1. **You move.** This will require you to figure out what's more important to you, living where you are or buying a home.

2. **You stay.** Continue living where you are, but buy a home in a less expensive area to get into the real estate market.

Just because you live in an area that's super expensive doesn't mean your home also needs to be in the same area. You can continue renting where you are and buy a home somewhere more affordable. Then, you can rent it out and get the benefits of renting in an expensive city and owning a home/building equity.

Pro Tip: Please don't use this idea and buy a cottage. Cottages are almost always bad ideas. The value of a cottage typically doesn't go up the same way, and they can be more volatile when it comes to the markets (when the economy is bad and people need money, they sell their cottages/second homes first). Cottages can also be super difficult to sell (taking months longer than a typical residential property in the surrounding area).

SHOULD I GO INTO DEBT FOR MY WEDDING?

I'm going to say this quite simply: No. Your wedding is one day, and it goes by *fast*. Does this mean you can't have a "lavish affair," if that's what you want? Also no.

It does mean you will need to plan for it. The average cost of a wedding in North America is almost $30,000—that's no small chunk of change.[52]

If you put this entire cost on credit, you can expect to pay:

- 10 percent, or $32,000 in interest spread over eighteen years, making the minimum $280 a month payment.

Or:

- 20 percent, or $176,000 in interest spread over thirty-six years, making the minimum $463 a month payment.

This means, on the low end, your wedding just cost you $60,000, and on the high end, it cost you just over $200,000.

The wedding industry is one of the worst for pushing tradition and societal expectations in terms of what you *have* to do:

- You *have* to send out physical save-the-dates, invites, and thank-you cards.

- You *have* to get them designed.

- You *have* to have all the expensive parties, like an engagement party, bridal shower, etc.

- You *have* to invite your mom's second cousin's grocery clerk's sister.

- You *have* to have an expensive wedding cake.

---

52 simplyelegantcorp.com/blog/average-wedding-cost-canada/.

- You *have* to buy a brand-new dress.

- You *have* to have a plated dinner.

- You *have* to provide some weird gift to your guests like flower seeds, a jar of honey, or some other knick-knack you will be pressuring people to take so you don't get stuck carrying them all home.

You have to...you have to...you have to—I could go on and on. When I looked at the cost of a wedding and what it would mean for me financially, my fiancé and I decided we didn't want to spend $30,000 for one day. We had friends who spent over $100,000, and they didn't even remember their wedding because they were so busy greeting everyone. It was a whirlwind—a whirlwind that cost them over six figures... ouch.

We decided to forgo almost all the traditions (to my mom's extreme dismay: *You mean, you're NOT inviting my old district manager from fifteen years ago that you've never met to your wedding?*). We had a destination wedding with twenty-five people, so I could focus on those who really mattered to me. We enjoyed a week-long vacation with our closest family and friends, instead of a single day. I did my own hair and makeup. We had a buffet. We didn't send out paper invites. We sent out e-invites for free and got automatic RSVP responses that went directly into an Excel spreadsheet—please tell me how this is not better. And we didn't have a wedding cake. Later, when I mentioned this to friends as a way we saved money, they were astonished because they hadn't even noticed that we didn't have a cake! Overall, we spent just over $10,000, including my dress, the ceremony, the DJ, the venue, and trips. We got *an entire week* with the people we loved most (and even the freaking week flew by).

Does the cost of weddings mean you have to forgo the expensive traditions? No. But you need to make sure you're doing the traditions because *you* want to. Because they make *you* happy and you would rather spend your money on those things than something else (like a house, if that's a goal you have). And if you do decide you want to spend $30,000 on your big day? You better start planning for it now. The biggest mistake I see people make is waiting until they get engaged to save for their wedding.

But, Nicole, what if I don't end up getting married and I've saved all this money? Take a second and read that again. Is having a bank account stacked with cash really a bad thing? If you're planning on getting married someday, you need to start planning on how you're going to pay for it *today*.

Let's work backward:

If you need $28,000 and plan to get married around the age of twenty-seven, you would need to save:

- Age 27: $28,000 for that year or $2,333 a month
- Ages 25–27: $14,000 a year or $1,166 a month
- Ages 23–27: $7,000 a year or $583 a month
- Ages 20–27: $4,000 a year or $333 a month

And if you end up deciding that a wedding isn't of value to you, then you have a fat bank account that you can use for another life expense—a car, house, starting a business, going back to school, paying down some of your student loans, child-related expenses, time off from work to travel. The opportunities are endless—having money saved is rarely a bad thing.

SHOULD I BUY A HIGH-END VEHICLE ON FINANCING?

The short answer? No. When people buy something new like a car, it's exciting. They're thinking about how much fun they'll have driving it, how cool they'll look, or how it's something they've always wanted.

It's a status symbol.

It shows they're successful.

They'll be respected.

Interestingly enough, did you know that most wealthy people actually don't drive luxury vehicles?[53]

Cars are depreciating assets. Meaning as soon as you drive it off the lot, it's worth significantly less than what you just paid for it. And they continue to lose their value at rapid rates. New cars lose 20–30 percent of their value after the first year, and in five years they've lost 60 percent of their initial value.[54]

The wealthy know this, and they don't put their money into "assets" that are only going to steal their money—they put their money into assets that make them money. And a car is by far one of the worst places you can put your money. Imagine just throwing your money out the window of the car as you drive off the lot.

But, Nicole, so many rich people have nice cars. Sure, they do. Let's talk about it:

---

53   forbes.com/sites/joannmuller/2011/12/30/what-the-rich-people-really-drive/

54   thinkinsure.ca/insurance-help-centre/car-deprecation.html

1. **Outward appearances can be deceiving.** Many of these people are likely fake rich. I always ask, do you want to *look* rich or *be* rich? Many people who are fake rich may look like they have it all to the outside world, but they're drowning in debt.

2. **Others buy assets with assets.** The ones who *are* rich likely used their money to first buy assets (like stocks, businesses, and real estate), so now their assets fund their lifestyle—that is, the money they make through investing in things like businesses, stocks, and real estate pays for the things they buy.

The biggest difference between a wealthy mindset and a broke mindset is how they choose to spend their active income (the money earned from trading their hours for dollars). The wealthy mindset invests its active income into cash-flowing assets (investments), and these cash-flowing assets (i.e., stocks and real estate) in turn make them more money, so they can stop trading their limited life (hours) for dollars. The wealthy mindset then uses money from the cash-flowing assets (passive income) to fund its lifestyle.

When the wealthy-mindset people get to a point where they are making enough money to fund their lifestyle from their investments passively, that's when you might see them start going out and buying "luxury items."

The broke mindset, on the other hand, uses its active income to fund its lifestyle instead of investing it to make more money passively. As a result, the broke mindset misses out on its opportunity to create more income that doesn't require trading hours for dollars, ultimately sabotaging its chances at becoming wealthy.

Fun Fact: Flashy luxury items are usually made for people who want to *look* rich, not necessarily for those who *are* rich. Ever heard the saying, "Wealth whispers"?

This quote asserts that people who have money, who are truly wealthy, don't need to prove to others that they're rich through what they drive and what they wear. Luxury brand-name items are a loud and expressive statement, whereas the truly wealthy are confident, and assured of who they are without the "flash."

When you buy a car, you need to consider the cost of the car and other factors:

- **Insurance:** How much will it cost to insure a high-end vehicle compared to another? A newer model vs. an older one?

- **Repairs:** Is this make/model likely to break down? Is it expensive to fix? Can it be serviced by a common mechanic, or will it require specialty servicing?

- **Gas:** What type of gas does it require? What is the mileage like, and how does it compare in different environments and driving conditions?

- **Resale Value:** How much will this baby be worth when you go to sell it in the future?

Overall, we want to understand the total cost of ownership for the vehicle, not just the promo rates the dealer is advertising (which are almost always a lie).

I don't own a luxury car, but could I? Sure. I went to the Lexus dealership before I got my mom-mobile. I looked at the gorgeous all-white SUV with brown leather interior. I thought about how cool I could look driving around in this. But then I went to the Kia dealership and found almost the same car for half the price. The difference? It says "Kia" on the front.

When I factored in the additional insurance and total cost of ownership, it was about a six-hundred-dollar-a-month difference. I asked myself, *Would*

I get six hundred dollars a month's worth of happiness more out of the Lexus than the Kia? At first, maybe. The first few weeks, as it's still got that new-car smell. While I'm driving around in my new toy, feeling like, "I've made it."

But it would fade. It always fades. The level of utility (or happiness and enjoyment) I would get out of the Lexus, compared to the Kia, was not worth six hundred dollars a month to me. After a few months, it becomes just another car. I use it to get to work and run errands, and I'm doing the same thing in the Kia—but for six hundred dollars a month less, and I'm using that extra money to get me closer to my other goal.

SHOULD I SPEND MONEY ON MY CREDIT CARDS WHEN I DON'T HAVE THE CASH?

This is an easy one, so I'll let you answer this one before I do.

No.

When you spend money on your credit card to buy shit you don't have the money for, you're stealing from your future self. The you in five years or ten years is going to be like, *"Shit, Jenny! Why the hell did you have to buy so many sweaters?"*

When you're wondering why you can't afford a down payment on a home, and you feel like you're drowning in debt—not only are you stealing from your future self, but you're taking a loan for a pair of shoes. A loan. *Yes.* That is exactly what using a credit card is, but it's been normalized because "everyone is doing it." But remember what I said when I talked about the average person? We're not here to be average. If everyone is doing it, it's almost safe to say that you likely shouldn't.

If you don't have the cash to pay for your purchase, you don't buy it. It's as simple as that. Credit cards can be wonderful things, or they can be predatory and suck you dry. I make a couple thousand dollars a year by using credit cards that give me cash back and filtering all my expenses through them. They can also provide great consumer protection if you ever buy something and have a dispute with the merchant (the credit card company has your back). They can give you perks when you fly or travel. Or they can rip out your soul and make you trade the rest of your life to get it back. Your choice.

But, Nicole, I only put purchases on my credit card when I have an emergency. Yes, I can see how that would be useful. However, there's something very important to note about this method and others associated with it.

- A credit card is not an emergency fund.

- A line of credit is not an emergency fund.

- An emergency fund is an emergency fund.

Using your credit card as an emergency fund is a surefire way to put yourself into a vicious debt cycle that is hard to break. Give yourself grace as you're changing your habits today, but know you need to be making the conscious choice to get your emergency fund built in. You should have six to twelve months of bare-bones expenses in cash in a high-yield savings account for your emergencies—not a credit card with a 19 percent APY, because once you start digging that hole, it can be soul-crushing and bury you.

HOW CAN I USE MY CREDIT CARD TO WIN?

Credit cards are often regarded as evil by the personal finance community, but I think they can be great tools when used correctly. As I said, I make a couple thousand dollars a year by filtering all my expenses through my credit cards. That said, you need to be certain you're in the right mindset and have the right behaviors to make this work. When I spend money on my credit card, I pay off my balance biweekly, or sometimes even the same day.

If you're new to this and are going to spend on your credit card, my recommendation would be to pay the balance off the same day because, if you start carrying a balance, all those cashback dollars likely won't cover the interest you're paying (which is how they get you). If you're only spending on your credit card to get the rewards, and you have the cash to pay for the things you're buying, it shouldn't be a problem to go in same day and pay off the balance.

To win with credit cards, you need to outsmart the credit card company. How do we do this?

- Never carry a balance.

- Don't buy anything you don't already have the cash to pay off.

- Save an emergency fund of six to twelve months bare-bones cash (a credit card is not an emergency fund).

- Don't pay an annual fee for a credit card. There are great card options that don't charge anything.

SHOULD I PAY DOWN MY STUDENT LOANS FASTER?

This one isn't such a clear-cut answer. It really depends on your personal situation. I don't think anyone wants to have debt. I know there is a ton of shame that can come from having debt of any sort. Please don't feel shame over your student loans; they helped you get the education you needed to get the job you have today and provided you the ability to increase your earning potential.

Even if you spent your loans on things you're not feeling super proud about right now (I know I spent my fair share on margaritas and clothes), know that there's no going back in time, but we do have the ability to choose differently in the future.

In most cases, yes, allocating more money every month to paying down your student debt is a good idea. Debt can hold us back because it's money that is working against us. I've heard it a thousand times:

"I feel like it's crushing me."

"I'm so embarrassed."

"I know I need to get it gone, now."

Should you be embarrassed by your student debt? No, you shouldn't be. Here's why:

1. **You borrowed the money to better yourself.** There is a difference between an expense and an investment, and your student loans represent an investment into bettering your future.

2. **Not everyone had parents or support in paying for school.** Nonetheless, you still decided to go and make the investment into *bettering yourself.* Be proud of that.

3. **The person you are now needed the loan then.** Your student loans paid for an education that likely put you in a situation today to earn more money. Without the opportunity they afforded you, you might not be where you are today.

4. **Your debt is not a reflection of who you are personally.** You did the best you could at the time with the information you had, and that is commendable, not shameful.

5. **Beating yourself up about your debt keeps you in a spiral of shame.** What you tell the mind, it believes. So if you keep telling yourself that your actions are embarrassing, that you are bad for having this debt, or that you're going to be stuck in a hole of debt your entire life, then guess where you'll be? Exactly where you keep telling yourself you are.

Look at your debt for what it is and thank it for the opportunities it's given you. Then get to work formulating a plan to repay it. When you have a plan, the other shit doesn't matter because day by day and week by week, you are getting closer and closer to your goal. And if your plan doesn't work? Change the plan but not the goal. Plans are made to evolve.

There is no shame or blame that can propel you to be the highest and best version of yourself, so start showing yourself some compassion. You're on the right foot, that's why you're here today.

Now, are there some situations where you may not want to put extra money on your student loan to pay it down faster? Sure. Let's talk about it.

The average interest rate on student loans is 5.8 percent, and in personal finance, we typically want to put our money where it is going to have the biggest benefit. We figure this out by comparing the interest rates available to us.[55]

It's a game I like to call "Would You Rather?" Think of your money like little workers. Let's say you make $60,000 a year, that means you have 60,000 little workers that can go out and get shit done for you. Let's say you have an extra

---

55   educationdata.org/average-student-loan-interest-rate

$500 a month, or 500 workers, that you can either put toward your student loans (or other debt, as this principle is applicable there as well) or other goals like investing for retirement.

Would you rather have your little workers make 5.6 percent by paying off your student loans, or earn 8 percent through investing those same dollars? The game of "Would You Rather?" compares the two possible interest rates, and typically, wherever you're getting the higher rate is where you want to put your money. That said, personal finance is personal—just because it might make more sense numbers-wise to put more money into investments, if you *personally* feel better about paying down your debt, that's what you should do.

If your debt is preventing you from getting where you ultimately want to go in life, then you need to focus there first. This is all going to come down to goal-setting and prioritizing, which we'll discuss in more detail later.

Before you start dumping more money into your student loans, there are some other considerations that should come first.

1. Saving your emergency fund.
Before you start aggressively paying down your debts, first and foremost, I want you to have a baby emergency fund of a thousand dollars saved. Why? Because if we don't have anything saved for emergencies (and they are inevitable—remember to always expect the unexpected), then we are going to be stuck in a constant vicious cycle of paying down debt and then accumulating more. You first need to save your baby emergency fund, and then start working toward your full six- to twelve-month fund of *bare-bones* living expenses.

2. Saving a down payment for a house.
If buying a home is a goal you have, you're going to need to save up a pretty hefty sum in order to make your purchase a reality—and you could be tempted to stop paying down your student loans as aggressively to focus on

this goal. While you should never forgo paying down high-interest debt like credit cards to start saving for other goals, your student loans are typically comparatively low-interest.

In some areas, not getting into the housing market sooner rather than later could be a bad financial decision. Some areas have above-average housing price growth. When I bought my first home, the prices were going up 20 percent year over year. Let's look at what this could mean for a $500k house:

Year 1: House is $500,000

Year 2: House is $600,000

Year 3: House is $720,000

That means the price of the house we wanted to buy was increasing by six figures a year—yikes! Now this is an extreme example, but let's look at something a little more realistic for many people, taking into consideration the type of growth we've seen in North America over the last decade.

Housing prices are increasing at 7 percent year-over-year:

Year 1: House is $500,000

Year 2: House is $535,000

Year 3: House is $572,450

This means that, every year, the price of the average $500,000 house is going up by $35,000. This also means that, if you aren't saving $35,000 a year, you're falling behind, and if you did manage to save $35,000 a year, you're just at par—meaning you're no further ahead than if you had bought in year one but you've had to save an extra $35,000 to be no further ahead.

In cases like these, it can make sense to jump in sooner rather than later to benefit from rising housing prices (instead of trying to fight against them). If buying a home is a goal of yours, you may want to consider allocating more of your income toward your down payment if the housing market is rising quickly to avoid getting into a situation where you are effectively priced out of the market or paying much more than you needed to for your property.

Caveat: If your "student loans" are actually credit card loans in disguise, with interest rates of 10–15 percent and above, those need to be focused on first.

HOW MUCH SHOULD I BE SAVING FOR RETIREMENT?

People in their twenties and thirties rarely think about saving for retirement. Most people wait until they're in their late forties and then have a freak-out moment, thinking, *Holy crap, how will I ever stop working?* Don't be that person. What people in their twenties and thirties don't realize is that time is on their side and that the earlier you get started, the less money you have to put in. Yes, you read that right: *the less money you have to put in.*

This is possible through the power of compound interest. For example, if you start saving $250 a month at twenty years old, investing earning approximately 8 percent growth per year, at sixty-five you would have over $1,200,000 in the bank (on average, for simplicity's sake, you can expect anywhere from 7 to 10 percent growth annually in the stock market). Of that $1,200,000, $1,060,000 was growth—meaning you contributed about $140,000 and made over a million dollars in free money. If you waited until you were forty to start, contributing at the same rate ($250 a month with 8 percent interest), you would have $227,000—or simply put, *a million dollars less*. Your total growth (a.k.a free money) would be just over $800,000, meaning that you missed out on $200,000 by waiting to start. If you wanted to retire with $1,200,000 in the bank, starting at forty, you'd need to contribute over $1,400 a month, or $16,800 a year. Talk about a buzzkill.

You should not be asking, "Should I start saving for retirement?"— that's a broke question. You should be asking "How much should I be saving for retirement?" The only time you will want to pause or slow down your retirement savings is if you have high-interest debt, like a credit card. Remember, put your money where it's going to get the highest return. If you can make 8 percent through a retirement account, but you're paying 19 percent-plus on your credit card, pay off the card first.

There is one exception to this rule: employer retirement savings matching. If your employer offers a match through your 401(k) or RRSP, contribute there first to get the free money. If your employer offers you a dollar-for-dollar match, that is an automatic 100 percent return on your investment (this could take seven to ten years in the stock market to earn, and you're getting it *automatically*), *plus* the potential 7–10 percent you can earn through investing those dollars in your investment account. If someone is offering free money, take it.

We'll talk more about how to determine what you personally should be saving for retirement in another section. There are some common rules that some experts recommend, but I don't think they work for everyone, as they focus on saving a percentage of your income (10–15 percent). I don't think this gives you an accurate way to plan—maybe 15 percent is too little for the lifestyle you want to live, or maybe it's too much. The only way to know how much we should save today is to look at our goal in the future, see how much it's going to cost us, and then work backward.

Overall, shifting from asking broke questions (which just keep you stuck) to asking wealthy mindset questions can have a huge impact on your finances. By now recognizing when you're getting stuck asking broke questions, you'll help prevent yourself from falling into analysis paralysis—which will help you start taking action, and just *doing the damn thing.*

Remember: A step in the right direction, no matter how "small," is still a step in the right direction. It will also help you start to focus on the bigger-picture items that have a real impact on your financial health.

CHAPTER 7

GETTING YOUR PARTNER **ON BOARD** WITH **YOUR GOALS**

I grew up watching my mom be responsible for all of the financial matters—she balanced the checkbooks (way back when checkbooks were a thing), she paid the bills, and she decided "what we had the money for." I don't think my dad had any clue what was going on.

You'd think a setup like this might be better for organization purposes (like, don't have too many cooks in the kitchen?), but in my experience it definitely was not. If you're in a partnership, you're supposed to be partners, and partners work *together*. Partners have shared goals. If one partner is completely freaking clueless, how on earth are they supposed to be effectively working toward building your dream life together? Short answer, they won't be.

From a financial perspective (and probably just life perspective overall), you should be thinking of your romantic partner like they are also your business partner. They're co-owner of The Hamiltons, Inc. (or whatever your last names are). Business partners need to be on the same page, they need to be working toward the same goals—otherwise, you're going to have disharmony in the business. Problems will arise, tensions will be high, and things won't get done the way they're supposed to, likely causing the relationship—*ahem* business partnership—to break down.

And when things aren't running smoothly, that's when goals don't get achieved, money doesn't get made, and businesses ultimately fail.

Many businesses fail and dissolve because of bad partnerships. Maybe one partner puts more money into the business than the other to keep it running and this causes resentment; maybe the other is bad with money and is always spending it before it comes in. Maybe one doesn't consult the other before making decisions that impact the business, and therefore impact both partners' ability to reach their personal and professional goals. Just like a partner in business, your romantic partner can help you achieve new financial heights by reinforcing good behaviors and pushing you toward your goals, but they can also be detrimental to your success if they're not on the same page.

How can a partner negatively impact you financially? In a number of ways, but the most common ones I've seen with our students and in my own personal life are:

- Not contributing to savings or investing goals

- Spending money that was allocated to goals on things other than goals, pulling you further back

- Not contributing to the household financially, so you need to make up for their lack of financial contribution to everyday expenses before you can start working toward your goals (extending your timeline to reach them, or making them difficult to hit)

- Not working, which could cause financial stress on the household

- Unilaterally making large purchases without agreement on how that impacts the goals of the household

- Hiding spending (financial infidelity)

- Taking on debt for consumerism (in many instances I've seen one partner spending frivolously on their credit card, and the other partner having to step in to pay the debts as they are negatively affecting the household)

All of these can prevent you from living the life you want, and can cause major turmoil in a relationship (money problems are cited as one of the major causes of divorce). Whether that's having opposing views on money, having financial infidelity in the relationship (yes, this kind of infidelity is just as serious—think of hiding spending, debts, loans, and other "behind-your-back" behavior that has the potential to derail a relationship), no compromises on spending, or even complications that can arise from simply combining bank accounts.[56]

This is because, although money isn't everything, everything takes money. Money isn't happiness in and of itself, but it provides you the means to live life true to your values; it is the means by which you can achieve your goals. So it might not *be* happiness, but you can use it to *create* happiness. So what do you do if your partner isn't on the same page as you financially, and refuses to change or become more financially responsible?

Do you marry for love, or do you marry for the life that you want? And I don't mean this in some sort of gold-digger way—I'm asking you to seriously consider if love really does conquer all. Because I don't want to tell you the number of times I have seen personally, and with our community of students, people in bad situations they didn't put themselves in, or people in relationships they don't want to be in (or need to get out of), but are stuck in.

---

56 spectrumfamilylaw.ca/blog/2019/12/30/money-financial-reasons-couples-get-a-divorce/.

COMMIT TO CHANGE

When you knowingly commit your life to someone, you are committing *your life to them*. You are committing to a certain lifestyle, based on their own personal values and goals—and if you're not on the same page from the beginning, and they're not willing to change, guess what happens?

You have two options:

1. Change your expectations, or

2. Change your life.

You either have to change and accept that this is the life you have, or you have to change it—and we can't change other people, so that strategy is off the table. So maybe that means working toward your financial goals in your relationship completely on your own.

Let's look at an example. Let's say buying a house is really important to you. You value security and freedom, and you believe that buying a house helps you live in alignment with those values. To buy a house, you know you have to come up with a good chunk of money for the down payment, closing costs, and cushion. You've been diligently saving money from your paychecks every two weeks toward your goals, but your partner isn't. You have to keep asking them to contribute to the goal, and sometimes they do, but most of the time asking them to contribute just causes a fight.

They're spending their money in other, frivolous ways, and they've made it very clear that they're happy renting. Buying a home for them isn't important, even though it's important to you. Maybe you've made it clear how important home ownership is to you, you've asked them to change their spending habits, but they just won't. If they do, it gets better for a couple weeks, and then it's back to the same shit. You can't change other people. For someone to change, they have to want to change, and it's very apparent to you that your partner doesn't want to. So at this point you can either change your expectations and maybe let go of your goal, or you can decide to work toward it solely on your own without their assistance.

This isn't something I would recommend, as being on opposite pages from your partner (especially when it comes to finances) can be a recipe for disaster. However, if you're truly happy staying in your relationship knowing you're alone in working toward your financial life goals, the way forward with this option would involve setting firm financial boundaries with your partner. The biggest mistake we can make with this approach is not setting a boundary and just expecting or assuming your partner will figure it out on their own. Even if they refuse to be on the same page as you financially, they absolutely must ensure that they are clear (and respectful) of your personal needs, values, and goals.

Maybe you've decided that buying a new home is important to you, but your partner doesn't want to devote time, energy, or money to the process. You've decided (after much deliberation, consideration, and weighing your options) that the new home is absolutely a top priority for you, and you're happy (like actually happy, not just pretending to be) to work toward it on your own. Your partner is fine with that, but they don't want to participate.

What boundaries do you come up with?

In this example, we may want to set up boundaries to protect ourselves and personal space, emotions, time, energy, money and possessions.

Boundaries are not about being mean or ostracizing other people; they're about protecting yourself, and are necessary in any relationship (especially if you're in a situation where you're feeling overwhelmed, unsupported, used, or uncomfortable). Boundaries can help protect you from those feelings, and are necessary in any relationship.[57]

Determining your boundaries really comes down to understanding your values and your rights or needs.

Start by writing out the two aspects noted earlier, and brainstorm everything you can think of that falls under both categories in relation to the situation you are creating boundaries for. There is no right or wrong answer here, as boundaries will be specific to an individual person.

Values: You can use the list we came up with in an earlier section to help you determine when, where, or how your personal values are being encroached upon, or are not in alignment with your current situation. This will provide you with the information you require to start figuring out your needs.

> **For example:** I value encouragement, safety, security, freedom, and family—and given the situation, I may feel as though many of these are being challenged.

From here, we're able to start working out our rights and needs.

Rights and needs: non-negotiables required for you to thrive (for example, being happy, healthy, and safe—both mentally and physically)

> **For example:** I need positive encouragement from my partner when I'm working toward a goal. I have a right to be free to go after my personal goals

---

57   healthline.com/health/mental-health/set-boundaries#boundary-basics-and-benefits

Now that you understand which values are being challenged in your situation, and how they're impacting your personal rights and needs, you can then use that information to formulate your boundaries.

> **For example:** Although your partner does not want to be involved in the home-buying process (saving or shopping for the property), you can still set the boundary that they be supportive and encouraging to you while you work toward the goal (this goes into your need for positive encouragement, and value of encouragement).

You can also set the boundary that they not impede your ability to save and purchase the home, as you have indicated you have a right to be free to go after your personal goals.

Caveat: Although you can reach a financial goal on your own, if the goal impacts all parties in the partnership (such as buying a home), in my opinion, it's more important to get on the same page (and if you're not able to, ask why—and maybe take it up with a therapist). Partnerships are two-way streets—and I know that a lot of you reading this have different goals or financial acumen than your partners, but there comes a point when maybe love doesn't conquer all, especially if it means sacrificing the life you want, or having to do it all on your own anyway (just my two cents).

In contrast, a partner who is on the same page as you financially and is assisting in working toward shared goals can impact you positively. Here is a list of some of the most common ways:

· More symbiosis in the relationship

· Feeling more connected and supported

· Ability to reach goals faster than if you were doing it on your own

- Feeling of being on a team, which can help push you to keep working toward your goals

- Happiness in achieving your goals together

- Fulfillment from living life true to your values

Imagine if you were in business with someone who was on a completely different page and path than you. Let's say you and Bill opened a restaurant—but the only thing that was agreed upon in your business partnership was that you were opening a restaurant together. You didn't discuss any of the other details, and if you tried to, Bill just completely shut down. So you decide it's easier to each do your own thing, but together.

Bill decides he is opening a fine dining restaurant, but you decide you'd like to run a sub shop. While Bill is busy hiring a harpist to play during dinner, you're installing light-up white and red menus at the front of the restaurant. Bill is setting tables with cloth napkins and tablecloths, and you're buying tens of thousands of dollars' worth of cold cuts to make subs. Bill is bringing in a French chef, but you've already hired a seventeen-year-old to make sandwiches.

Your business isn't going to do very well because customers aren't going to have any idea what's going on—you're both working toward completely different goals. You're spending money on things that don't complement each other, and therefore you're going to have to keep spending money to redo what the other has already done. You will never have a thriving business because you're not on the same page as to what needs to happen and when.

Or we could look at this another way. Let's say you and Bill decide you're opening up a restaurant. You start making business plans, hiring staff, creating the menu, and decorating, but Bill couldn't be bothered. He doesn't show up to the meetings, doesn't listen when you try to discuss what's happening with him, and gives you no input on any of the decision-making because he just doesn't really care. The business is important to you, so you start clocking in more hours, putting in more energy, sinking in more of your money. Bill, on the other hand, shows up at the restaurant maybe once a week, and when he does, he just sits at the bar and has a beer. Sometimes he takes money out of the cash register to buy things without discussing it with you, and last week he took a loan out against the business without your knowledge to buy a new sports car.

Doesn't sound like it's going to be a very successful business or partnership, does it? But so many people are running their lives and relationships like this. One partner is doing all the heavy lifting, while the other sits back. Or both partners are heavy-lifting on their own, but neither is helping the other because they're not on the same page about where they want to go in life. If you relate to either of these messages, take this as a sign to get on the same page.

FOSTERING SHARED GOALS WITH YOUR PARTNER

It's clear that having shared goals and a shared life plan are necessary to have a happy and successful relationship—but if you're not currently on the same page as your partner, how do you get them on board?

1. First things first, we need to remember we cannot change anyone. A lot of us go into relationships thinking that just because something is a certain way right now, doesn't mean it will always be that way. Something I've learned over the years is: when someone shows you who they are, believe them. No matter how much nagging, asking, begging, or ultimatum-issuing you do, someone will never change unless they personally want to. You may see short-term results

with those kinds of actions, but it will continue to be a battle in your relationship until that person truly wants to change. And we need to realize that sometimes, that person may never want to "be who we want them to be."

2. The next thing to remember is that just because something is a value to us doesn't mean it's a value to someone else (and vice versa). You're allowed to have some different values than your partner—for instance, convenience is a big value to my husband. He is happy to pay more for things that make his life more convenient. Me, not so much. I would generally rather do more of the work myself and save my money for other things that I value more—and that's okay! As long as our overall values and goals in life are aligned (i.e., that we generally want to live life in a similar fashion), then having some values that are different is fine and normal.

   The problem I see a lot of people run into is that they try hard to change their partners' values instead of accepting them for what they are and understanding that they may not always want to spend money in exactly the same way—but that as long as your overarching life values and goals are aligned, the small differences are okay. If your vice is spending on higher-end cosmetic products because beauty is a value to you, but your partner would prefer to spend more on higher-end coffee—neither is wrong or bad, as long as you are both working toward your shared goals in life. If your values are all disproportionately different from your partner's, then yes, it may become difficult to get on the same page with goals, but more about that later.

3. When we're looking at the best way to get your partner on board with your own personal goals, one of the things I love to do is to show them how excited I am, how important it is to me, and how

it will impact/benefit them. Don't make it all about you if you want their buy-in.

4. A great way to get on the same page is with money dates—pick a date, make dinner, maybe have some wine, and sit and talk with your partner about your dreams, wishes, and goals. Ask them what they want in their life, and share what you want in yours. Make it fun—see not only how they can get on board with your dreams, but how you can get on board with their dreams as well.

5. Once you've gotten on the same page about your life goals, continue the money dates (make them fun) to think about how you can reach your goals, and start using them not only to dream, but to strategize: What do you have to do now to set yourself up for success?

6. Remember: No shaming or blaming for choices that are someone else's value. For example, my husband loves to drink coffee. I don't, and for me it would be a waste of money, but for him, it's not, and that's okay as long as it is not negatively impacting our ability to reach our shared goals.

7. Make it a point to start having more positive conversations around money (the money dates are great for these), because if the only time you're ever talking about money is when you're fighting, or it's in a negative context, just the thought of it will cause anxiety and strain on your relationship.

8. Remember to show them how serious you are about your personal financial goals—there are tons of people who talk about things they want to do but never go out and do them. Show your partner this is something you truly want, and that you're willing to do the work and make the necessary changes to get there.

> › **Pro Tip:** complete some research and preemptively think about their questions, hesitations, or concerns before you talk about it, so you can show how prepared and serious you are.

9. Be willing to try new things with your partner as well—maybe they have goals they'd like to pursue; will you support them? Show them, and that can make reciprocation easier.

Now, what if you try this and your partner won't get on board, or refuses to change their financial habits that are negatively impacting your relationship or shared goals (like financial infidelity, not working, or going into consumer debt)? If it's a relationship you stay in, be ready to protect yourself if they refuse to be financially responsible. This means not cosigning loans or leases, not putting your name on shared accounts or credit cards, and keeping your money separate. If you're coming into the relationship with assets (think cars, homes, investments or savings), you may even want to consider a prenup.

If your partner refuses to get on board with your goals, ask yourself how you feel about that. You can try to show and explain to them how it hurts you emotionally that you're not working toward the goals together, but remember Point One: You can't change someone else. If your partner refuses to get on board, are you happy to go after the goals yourself, or is it important for you to have someone on your team who shares the same goals? If you decide you're happy to work toward the goals alone, you need to remember that this was your choice (because we cannot change people) and you need to find happiness in the choice (or else you'll drive yourself crazy with resentment).

CHAPTER 8

SAVING IS ONLY PART OF THE BATTLE

I had a friend in high school who had a job in a nursing home, so she made more on an hourly basis than myself and most of my other friends, who largely worked in fast-food restaurants as teenagers. Her parents didn't want her to spend all of this money she was making, so they used to take half of it and put it away for her—I remember she was somewhat upset about it because she didn't have it all available to spend (on the stupid crap we bought as teenagers), but that she wasn't entirely mad because she knew they were using it to set her up for success financially in the future.

For a long time, I believed that saving money was simply having money left over in my checking account before my next paycheck came in, and that sometimes people saved money when they wanted to purchase something big, if they made really good money and could afford it—like a trip or a new car. That was the norm while I was growing up.

Throughout my personal finance journey, I realized I had created the following internal beliefs and rules about saving:

- Saving was only possible if you made good money (more than the average person)

- The only time you saved money was when you wanted to buy something

- Not everyone saved money, but if you did, you were really good with it

The gold standard in life became: Make lots of money, and if you can afford it, save some—then you'll be good with money. I truly thought that wealthy people were people who just made lots of money (through working, or getting lucky through something like an inheritance or lottery win) and saved it all in their bank account. And based on my experience, this idea emerged that saving money in and of itself is enough to make you good with money, and make you financially secure—however, this couldn't be further from the truth.

- Saving money is not enough to be good with money.

- Saving money is not enough to make you wealthy.

- Saving money alone will not be enough to create financial security in your life.

- Saving money isn't the key to becoming financially free or owning your time.

- Saving money alone won't provide you the means to retire.

THE RETIREMENT SAVINGS MYTH

Did you know that it is said the average American makes $1,600,000 in their lifetime, but experts say the average American will also need approximately $1,700,000 to retire?[58] That means that, even if you saved

---

58 cnbc.com/2019/08/11/what-is-the-magic-retirement-number-try-1point7-million.html

every dollar you ever made (which is impossible, since we need money to live), you wouldn't have enough to retire. Now, this may come as a surprise to many of you, because I also believed that for a long time—but retirement is not an age. I thought that, at sixty-five, you got to stop working no matter what. Unfortunately, that's another lie we've been sold by society, because retirement isn't an age, it's a number in the bank—or a number invested, to be more exact. When we hit that number, we get to retire—no matter how old we are. And if we never hit that number, well, then we don't get to stop working, because everyone needs money to live.

How do we hit this number? Not by saving, but by investing. By growing our money without our physical input. You see, when you're always trading hours for dollars, or time for money, there will always be a limit to how much you can make. There's a limit to how much time you have available to trade for money (there are only twenty-four hours in a day), and there's a limit to how much you can personally earn on an hourly basis—look at the top salary ranges for someone with your education, background or skill set: there's always a cap. The wealthy don't get wealthy by working more, or simply saving more money. To really build wealth, your focus should not just be on saving more, but on learning how to make money while you sleep. That's the real way to build wealth.

I used to believe that, to make more money, I had to work more—for a while I held multiple jobs. I thought that trading more hours of my life, and saving that money, were enough to create financial freedom. And while it did provide me with more financial security, it wasn't enough to really move the needle in a way that would truly change my life. Just earning more isn't enough to build wealth—it's not just about dollars in, it's about dollars out, and dollars grown. For example, you are not automatically rich when you become a doctor or lawyer. You may *earn* more money than the average person, but what you do with your money matters more than how much you bring in. You can be broke making $100,000 a year, and rich making $40,000 a year—it's all about what you do with it.

I didn't become a millionaire by physically earning a million dollars, by trading each hour of my life for money that added up to a million dollars. I became a millionaire by *growing* a million dollars through the power of investing—big difference. Many of us believe that millionaire status is something that is impossible for most people, because to get that kind of money you need to "strike it rich"—either by having wealthy family that you inherit the money or a business from, or through something like winning the lottery. The thing most of us don't realize is that 88 percent of millionaires are actually self-made—meaning they had no help and no handouts; they did it on their own (and it's actually a lot easier than you think).[59]

If we're talking about becoming a millionaire simply by saving more money, it's true: it's likely not going to happen. You'd need to save over four thousand dollars per month to reach millionaire status in twenty years, which is an impossible feat for most people. But what if I told you that making the right decisions from an earlier age could set you up to become a millionaire with only a hundred dollars a month? That you didn't need to save hundreds of thousands of dollars to become wealthy, or even retire decades earlier than most? We aren't taught this in middle-class households—but this education can make all the difference. We're taught that saving some money is the golden ticket, but most of us never get exposed to anything beyond that.

The way I see it is, whether you like it or not, forty-five years of your life has been sold to the economy. From the time you are twenty until you're sixty-five, you're expected to work, to contribute, to be a cog in the machine. This is why we're pushed into spending tomorrow's dollar, because if tomorrow's dollar is always spent, we always have to keep working and pushing. When you learn to stop spending tomorrow's dollar, you can begin to bring some stability back into your life—missing work

---

59   money.usnews.com/money/blogs/on-retirement/articles/7-myths-about-millionaires

for a day or two doesn't throw you into a complete financial disaster, but you still have to show up regularly or else you wouldn't be able to sustain your lifestyle.

When you learn to save, and not just avoid consumer debt, then you get to have a little more stability, a little more safety, a little more freedom. If you lost your job for a short period of time, or needed to take unpaid time off for medical leave, you'd probably be okay, but you'd have to go back to work to replenish those savings, because they only last for so long. But when you learn to not just save, but invest your money, you get to start buying some of your life back.

MAKING YOUR MONEY WORK FOR YOU

When you employ your money and not just yourself, when you put your money to work, it has the ability to work harder than you do—because money doesn't need a break. It doesn't need days off. It doesn't have a dentist appointment at five o'clock. Money can work for you 24/7, 365, but only if you tell it what to do. This is what happens when you invest: you employ your dollars.

Too many of us have it backward—we're employed, and our money (if we're "good" with money) is sitting in our savings account *unemployed*. Our money is relaxing, while we're out working hard. The key to being good with money isn't having it wasting away in your savings account; it's employing it, putting it to work for you, that will allow you to start to relax. When you invest your money, you start to reduce the number of years you need to trade for money—because, remember, your money can work harder than you can; it can grow exponentially and multiply faster than you can work for it trading hours for dollars. This is how people become wealthy and successful financially: they invest their money in income-producing assets that provide them with cashflow, and then use that money to fund their lifestyle.

We do things differently in the middle class, and this small change can be the difference between working forever and finding wealth and financial freedom. In the middle class, we work for money, and we use that money to buy the things we want—the house, the clothes, the cars, the technology, the shoes. We trade hours of our lives for dollars, and then we use that money to buy *things*. Once we've spent the money on the things, that's it—the money is gone.

People with a wealthy mindset do it differently. They work for money, trade hours for dollars, and then use that money to buy income-producing assets. They buy businesses, stocks, and real estate. They use their money to buy things that make them money—they multiply their dollars. So they've worked for money, and then spent the money, but that money will continue to come back to them over and over and over again. When their assets (the things they've bought) provide them enough money, they use that money to fund their lifestyle. Then they may choose to buy the shoes, and the clothes, and the cars. They're not using the money they've worked for to buy those things, they're using the free money that's been generated by the assets they've purchased. When you make that shift, that's how you can buy your life back.

That's how I started to buy my life back. Instead of spending money on consumer goods, I started investing that money into stocks and real estate. With my first real estate purchase, I turned a $15,000 investment into $150,000. That's a tenfold return on my investment. That's $150,000 that I got without having to trade my time for it. For me to simply *save* $150,000 would have taken me years and a lot of work, whereas by learning how to invest, I made that money with little to no extra effort—all while I was still working, earning money, and building up other investments.

Imagine if you had been taught about the powers of not just saving, but investing, from a young age. If we had thought about our dollars not as dollars, but as little workers. I want you to start looking at money this way—that you aren't earning $40,000 or $60,000 or $100,000 a year; you have 40,000 or 60,000 or 100,000 little workers. You're the boss, and you need to tell these workers what to do. Are you going to let them chill in your checking account, or are you going to put them to work? And the earlier you learn how to put them to work, the better, because this is where compound interest really starts to do its thing.

IN THE INTEREST OF TIME

As Albert Einstein says, compound interest is the eighth wonder of the world. **Compound interest** is when your money makes you more money, and then you make more money on the free money, and the growth of free money from free money becomes exponential.[60]

Ever heard the riddle, "Would you rather have a million dollars today, or a penny doubled every day for thirty days?" From the outset, most people would be like, uh yeah, give me the million...but those people would be missing out on over four million by not choosing the penny option. This is all due to the power of compounding. If you had a single penny and doubled it every day for thirty days, you would have $5,368,709.12—and no, that's not a typo. The craziest thing about this is that, if we changed the riddle to say twenty-seven days instead of thirty, you would only have $671,088.64. This is because the way investing works, the way compounding works, is that the more time you have for your investments to grow, the harder they can work for you. This is how people can build

---

60   breezejmu.org/business/compound-interest-the-eighth-wonder-of-the-world/article_11a24ebe-9e77-11eb-ba00-33aaec328747.html.

insane levels of wealth with smaller-dollar investments, just by getting started and giving their money more time to grow and work for them.

Most conventional wisdom will tell you that to build wealth, you need a lot of cash, but that's just not the case. **Time is more important than money when it comes to investing.**

- Starting at age twenty, if you invested a hundred dollars a month into the stock market, you could have over $1,126,000 at the traditional age of retirement.

- If you started investing five hundred dollars a month from the age of twenty-five until thirty-five, you could have approximately $100,000. Even if you never saved another dollar, by leaving this $100,000 invested, you could have over $1,700,000 at the traditional age of retirement.

- Investing two hundred dollars a month, starting at twenty, until you were thirty, could give you approximately $40,000. Leaving this $40,000 invested and never saving or investing another dollar could give you over $1,124,000 at sixty-five.

- If you started investing five hundred dollars a month at twenty, you could retire a millionaire at fifty years old—that's fifteen years earlier than the average. You would have gotten over $850,000 in *free* money (growth) to get to that million dollars, meaning you would have only put in just over $150,000.

Making these decisions to get your money working for you earlier in life can set you up for a lifetime of financial success, and can be the key to building wealth without having to work more or work harder for it. Money you save and invest in your twenties is worth twice as much as money you save and invest in your thirties due to compound interest. But if you're in your thirties or later reading this—it's not "too late" for you. Many of our students didn't start investing until after their thirties, and they've still set themselves up to live well and reach their financial goals!

If your goal is to retire at sixty-five with a million dollars in the bank (which could provide you with approximately $40,000 a year in cash to live off of without risk of running out of money), here's how much you would need to invest, starting at different ages, assuming a 10 percent annual return (based on the average annual return of the stock market over the last hundred years):

Age 25: $200 a month would get you to $1,100,000

Age 30: $300 a month would get you to $1,019,000

Age 35: $500 a month would get you to $1,031,000

Age 40: $850 a month would get you to $1,048,000

Age 45: $1,400 a month would get you to $1,005,000

Age 50: $2,500 a month would get you to $996,000

The less time you give your money to work for you, the more you would have to personally contribute to get the same benefit. Stop waiting for the perfect time to implement this, and start taking action now so your money can work for *you*.

But, Nicole, who knows if I'll live long enough to spend it? I should enjoy today. This is a common argument I hear about saving for retirement. While there's a multitude of things wrong with that statement, the three main factors are:

1. **North Americans today are living longer thanks to advances in technology, science, and medicine.** Men have a 90 percent chance and women have a 93 percent chance of living to age seventy.[61] Using YOLO as an excuse not to plan for retirement is statistically incorrect, and quite honestly hoping to die young so you don't have to plan for getting older is a dreary and dark way to live. The likelihood is you are going to get old, so you can pretend it's not going to happen to you and live out your senior years in poverty, or you can take action steps today to ensure you're taken care of. Nearly one in ten seniors live in poverty,[62] and your government support is not enough to get you through. You're still going to be a person when you're sixty-five; set yourself up for success today—it's easier than you think.

2. **Saving for tomorrow and investing for retirement is not depriving yourself.** You don't have to restrict yourself to save money, and by learning to invest, you can put aside even a small amount of money that can grow exponentially over time. Remember: we don't want to have an all-or-nothing attitude. Start where you can, make adjustments, reverse-engineer your goals, and live true to your values. This is why investing early and often is one of the money rules that will help you build out your best life.

3. **You don't have to wait until you're old to enjoy your money.** By learning how to invest early, and making financial freedom a priority, many people working regular everyday jobs have been able to retire decades earlier (some even in their thirties!). Remember: Life is what you make it, and retirement is a number in the bank, not an age.

---

61 hamiltonproject.org/charts/probability_of_a_65_year_old_living_to_a_given_age_by_sex_and_year

62 acl.gov/sites/default/files/Aging%20and%20Disability%20in%20America/2020ProfileOlderAmericans.Final_.pdf

What I need you to take from this chapter is that saving in and of itself is never going to be enough to get you where you want to go in life, and that your money can work harder than you ever can—so learn how to put it to work. Just leaving your money in your savings account means you are in fact losing money, and this is due to our little friend inflation. **Inflation** occurs when the general cost of goods and services increase over time. Ever heard your parents complaining about how much milk or gas costs today? You can thank inflation for that. We can expect an average of 2–3 percent inflation every year, meaning the cost of things we buy will go up by 2–3 percent annually, or also meaning that, if our money is sitting in a savings account and not growing, it's losing 2–3 percent of its value every year.

This is why we keep our emergency fund (which should *always* be in cash) in a high-yield savings account—because it's not safe to invest it (we need it available in cash in an emergency), so we want to fight inflation and loss of value as much as possible. A good HYSA will give you somewhere around 2 percent interest, but the rates fluctuate with what's going on in the economy. For our longer-term goals, that's why we must invest— because not only can our money work harder for us, and not only is it the real way to build meaningful wealth, but we also need to fight against inflation and having our savings lose value over time.

Two super easy ways to get your money working for you, grow your money, and fight inflation?

1. Open a HYSA for your short-term goals and emergency fund— look for one with no or low fees, that's CDIC- or FDIC-insured (so your money is safe), and that has good customer service ratings or reviews

2. Start investing in the stock market (this is not as hard or as scary as you think)

CHAPTER 9

GROW YOUR MONEY IN THE STOCK MARKET

We now know that getting your money to work for you is imperative not only for building wealth, but also for building financial stability and security in the future. We also know that the way investing works is that we give it either more time, or more money. Don't want to contribute a lot of money to get started (or don't have a lot to start with)? No problem, give your investments more time to compound and work for you. If you have a shorter time frame available before you need the money, or you want to fast-track your results (for example, if you were interested in pursuing early retirement), then you could add more money.

There are quite a few ways to invest your money to get it growing. Some of my personal favorites (and ones that I've used to grow my net worth and passive income) are:

- **Stocks**—where you own a small piece of a company (by purchasing a stock, you become a part owner of that company)

- **ETFs** (exchange traded funds)—these are like baskets of stocks. By purchasing an ETF, you can become part owner in hundreds or thousands of companies at once

- **Bonds**—this is where you lend out your money to companies or the government, and get paid interest

- **REITs** (real estate investment trusts)—these are companies that own real estate, and share their profits with you (great way to invest in real estate without becoming a landlord)

- **Private Lending** (in Canada these are referred to as **MICs**—mortgage investment corporations)—these are my favorite for passive income. You pool your money with other investors and provide mortgages to people or businesses (I personally only lend to people under certain criteria and never do 1:1 loans)

- **Real Estate**—where you own a property and seek to make money from appreciation (how much the property increases in value), or through collected rents

Each type of investment comes with its own nuances, so for the purposes of this book (and the ease of you getting started), we're going to focus on the simplest ways to build wealth through the stock market!

Now, I know just hearing the term "stock market" can be intimidating. I too, for a long time, believed stocks were just for old white men in suits screaming into phones, and that good investing meant having some sort of insider knowledge of what company was going to be the next big thing. I thought it was a sort of gambling that only the super-rich could afford, and you could strike it big, like the lottery, or lose everything. In actuality, that's not an accurate representation of the stock market, what investing should be like, or how risky it is.

Let's start off by getting a clear understanding of what the stock market actually is. Simply put, the **stock market** (or stock exchange) is where buyers and sellers go to connect and buy or sell investments. That's it—it's not some super scary thing. It's literally just the medium of exchange for investors to go and buy or sell their investments.

Oftentimes, there are myths that overshadow what the stock market is, and internal beliefs that shape our understanding of, and willingness to engage in, investing.

INVESTMENT MYTHS

In my experience, some of the most prevalent **myths** are:

- You need to be rich to invest

- Investing is like gambling

- You absolutely need a financial advisor

- You need a large sum of money to get started

- Investing is difficult and scary

Now, let's dispel them.

- **Myth One: You need to be rich to invest.**
  As we talked about in earlier chapters, investing is how you become rich, not the other way around. We know that you can invest small amounts of money and see big results due to the power of compound interest, and that the earlier you get started, the less money you have to contribute to see big results. Investing is not something that you do once you get rich, it's how you build wealth and become rich.

- **Myth Two: Investing is like gambling.**
  The people who say investing is like gambling either 1) have never invested before, and are just perpetuating something they've heard, or seen, but potentially did not understand, or 2) think that trading and investing are the same thing.

  According to Merriam-Webster, gambling is "the practice or activity of betting, the practice of risking money or other stakes in a game or bet."[63] Wikipedia also defines gambling as "the wagering something of value [money] on an event with an uncertain outcome with the intent of winning something else of value."[64] I want you to remember part of the sentence—*with an uncertain outcome*—while I provide some more background and context.

  So if there are two main reasons why someone would consider investing to essentially be gambling, with one reason being the person's inability to distinguish between trading and investing, we'll need to further define those. **Trading** is the act of buying and selling investments in a short period of time. Trading is what comes to mind for most people when they think of investing and the stock market. The image I shared at the beginning of the chapter, with the old white men in suits screaming at TVs and on the phone? Those aren't people who are investing; they're trading. They're buying and selling stocks over a short period of time. They're trying to get rich quick. They're the ones trying to find the hottest new company to invest in, and then throwing all their money in, hoping that *this is the one that helps them strike it rich.*

  People think that, to make money in stocks, you have to be a trader—but that actually couldn't be further from the truth. In

---

63 merriam-webster.com/dictionary/gambling
64 en.wikipedia.org/wiki/Gambling

actuality, studies show that traders lose money. A study of eToro day traders found nearly 80 percent of them had lost money over a twelve-month period. Another study of day traders in Taiwan between 1995 and 2006 found only 5 percent of day traders had made money. And lastly, a study by the US Securities and Exchange Commission of forex traders found 70 percent lose money every quarter on average, and traders typically lose 100 percent of their money within twelve months.[65]

The difference between trading and investing is that investors take a long-term, diversified, get-rich-slow-and-steady approach. This contrasts with traders, who take a short-term, concentrated, get-rich-quick approach. The stock market is volatile in the short term—stock prices can change hundreds of times a day. Making money in the short term is purely luck—like gambling. But with investing, and a long-term diversified approach (more on this later), the stock market is a proven medium to create wealth, and shows consistent performance over the long term. Which essentially means, while in the short term we don't know what we're going to get (which is why short-term day traders usually lose money), in the long term, results become more predictable. Just as time is key in growing your money with compound interest, time is also key in reducing your risk with investing.

In fact, Vanguard completed a study that looked at historical stock market returns and your risk of losing money over various periods of time. The study says, "Based on past history, if you invested in the stock market for one year, your chance of losing money would be greater than one in four. But if you invested for ten years, that

65 markets.businessinsider.com/news/stocks/if-you-re-day-trading-you-will-probably-lose-money-here-s-why-1030667770

number would drop to about one in twenty-five—and after twenty years, to zero."[66]

Now, can you recall what I asked you to remember about the definition of gambling? That gambling is, "the wagering something of value [money] on an event *with an uncertain outcome* with the intent of winning something else of value."[67] Based on this definition, 100 percent yes, trading is gambling. It's like taking your life savings down to the casino and throwing them on black. Maybe you walk out stinking rich, maybe you lose your shirt—the outcome is uncertain.

But if we look at investing with a long-term strategy, and over a twenty-year timeframe, we can see that, according to this study and historical returns in the stock market, with the right strategy, we could reduce that risk to zero. With inflation at 2–3 percent (or more) per year, stagnant wages, and a limit to how much we can make if we're always trading hours for dollars, it seems like the bigger gamble is actually not investing at all. The easiest way to get rich is to pick low-cost, diversified investments (like ETFs) and then just leave them alone for thirty years—seriously, it's that simple (more on this soon).

· **Myth Three: You need a financial advisor to help you navigate investing.**
I myself believed this myth for a long time as well. I believed that the stock market was complicated, that investing was risky, and that I needed someone looking at my investments constantly so that they were safe. This is all incorrect.

---

66   investor.vanguard.com/investing/how-to-invest/risk-reward-compounding
67   en.wikipedia.org/wiki/Gambling

The stock market is actually quite simple once you get down to what's actually necessary to know—it's the people who day-trade that make it complicated, and I think we've established that's not the strategy we're going to be taking with our money if we want to be successful. We've also seen that, as long as you have the correct strategy, studies show you are much more likely to make money than lose it (especially if you're investing for the long term, like in the aforementioned Vanguard study). You also don't need someone "looking" at your investments all the time, as again studies actually show the more you touch your investments, typically the less money you make.

I truly believe that these myths are perpetuated by the financial services industry, because if you're scared of investing and believe it's too complicated to do on your own, then you'll keep hiring financial advisors and paying their exorbitant fees. And if you've ever looked into a financial advisor before, maybe you've seen fees in the range of 1–2.5 percent and thought, well that's really not that much. But just as your money can compound and grow for you, these fees can compound and grow against you. Just a 1 percent difference in fees could mean ten years less in retirement income. Ten years.[68]

Something else I hear a lot is that the financial advisor can create a better portfolio for you than you could create yourself, which again is just not factually correct. An actively managed fund sold to you by a financial advisor is not inherently better, and according to many studies, they actually perform worse. A study by S&P Global published in 2020 found that actively managed funds underperformed their respective index over a ten-year period

---

68   forbes.com/sites/robertberger/2021/02/05/how-a-1-investment-fee-can-wreck-your-
retirement/

(something you could have purchased yourself for a fraction of the cost). Furthermore, there have been countless lawsuits against actively managed funds who claim to be creating "a better portfolio than you could create yourself," when they're actually just creating you a portfolio based on an index, something you could buy on your own for less money, and then selling it to you for more.[69]

Don't even get me started on the fact that some financial advisors 1) are not **fiduciaries**, meaning they don't legally have to put your best interests first (which is a dangerous game when there are high commissions on the line), and 2) are salespeople first. Even if you find a financial advisor who is incredible, they still likely work for an institution that puts profits first.

Now, this isn't to pooh-pooh financial advisors; it's to help you open your eyes to the fact that, even if you choose to go to one, you still need to be educated and knowledgeable, and to not put blind faith in someone to exercise such control over your financial health, wealth, and future.

I found out a couple years ago that my dad received a pension from his job when he left, and, not knowing anything about investing, he went to the bank to ask them what to do with it. The advisor there told him to put the money into a GIC, a guaranteed investment certificate (in the US the equivalent would be a CD, or a certificate of deposit). GICs and CDs are known to be decent investments in the short term, because they're secure and don't fluctuate in value (meaning you won't lose money), but they also don't build wealth, because the returns generally don't keep up with inflation (they hover around 2 percent, depending on what's happening in the economy). Not knowing anything about investing, my parents

69 cbc.ca/news/canada/british-columbia/closet-indexing-expert-opinion-lawsuit-1.6185566

listened to the guy at the bank. It's now about twenty years later, and they'll need the money to retire in a few years. The investment is worth basically the same amount, whereas if they invested it, it could have grown by a half million dollars. They could have over $500,000 more today if they had put their money in the right place, if they had known about their options, if they hadn't listened to the guy at the bank. That's a half-million dollars that would have gone a long way in their retirement, that they can never make back now, because they cannot go back in time and let compound interest do its thing.

Can advisors be helpful? Sure, but not because they pick better investments than you could have picked yourself—it's because they can manage your emotions (so you don't make bad decisions, like buying high and selling low in a panic, or dumping all your money into a single company that you think is *going to the moon*), and because they can help you plan for things like taxes and retirement. Their value is in the extras, but you're paying an arm and a leg for it, and it's nothing that you couldn't do on your own.

If you are going to use a financial advisor, make sure you hire a fiduciary—I prefer fee-only (so they're not motivated by commissions, which could sway which investments they offer to you)—and educate yourself so you can sit at the table and have the conversation about your money and your future.

- **Myth Four: You need a large sum of money to get started with investing.**
  You absolutely do not—you could get started with five dollars if you wanted to. This is another myth that I believe is perpetuated by the financial services industry. I can't tell you how many messages I've gotten from people telling me they tried to start investing years

ago, but were told by a financial advisor they needed $20,000 to get started.

This is absolutely not true. What probably happened is the financial advisor didn't want to take on a client with a smaller portfolio, because it's just as much work to manage as a larger one, but instead of redirecting them to a platform that would allow them to invest with a smaller starting portfolio, the advisor just gave them a blanket statement that *it's not possible.* These statements prevent people from getting started, and can literally be the difference between them having enough money for retirement, or not.

Remember: If you don't have a lot of money to get started with, that's okay—give it more time and your money will compound and grow for you. Telling people they can't get started without $20,000 (which can be an astronomical sum for some) can dissuade them from ever trying, because they don't feel they can build up the $20,000. So then, by them not getting started when they can, the advisors have made it much more difficult for them in the future.

I'll say it again: Investing isn't for the rich, it's how you get rich.

- **Myth Five: Investing is difficult and scary.**
It's not—stop confusing your inexperience with inability. We as humans are born not knowing anything—have you seen a human baby? They can't even hold up their heads. If you weren't taught about money and investing, it's not your fault. If you're hearing something for the first time, yes, it's probably going to feel difficult or scary, because you don't have the experience. But I promise you, it is so much easier than you think.

Remember: Money is a skill. To learn a skill, we have to practice. So that might mean reading this chapter over a few times, taking notes, asking questions, doing more research, and that's okay! Not only is that okay, but it's normal! No one becomes an expert by doing something one time. It feels scary just because you've never done it before—but the more you do it, the more comfortable you'll get.

I was scared when I first started investing. I hired a financial advisor because I thought that's what you had to do. I truly believed he was doing something that I couldn't do on my own. That I needed someone "watching" my investments. That I would lose all my money if I tried, because it was hard to be successful. But that's wrong—and I'm going to teach you the most simple and effective way to grow your wealth with stocks. Yes, it will be easy, and yes, you will be able to implement it yourself.

So let's get into it—I want to talk in more detail about the different types of investments you can buy in the stock market, and the significance of each one.

SEVEN STOCK MARKET INVESTMENT TYPES

- **Stocks**—where you own a small piece of a company (by purchasing a stock you become part owner in that company). When most people think of investing in the stock market, buying stocks is what usually comes to mind—however, I personally don't invest in individual stocks. My thought process is that when you invest in one company, it's like gambling—you don't know what's going to happen in the long run. So instead of purchasing a single company and hoping it's good, I prefer to invest in hundreds or thousands of companies that represent the entire market. The key to being a good investor is investing for the long term, not making emotional decisions, and diversifying your investments (which simply means, don't put all your eggs in one basket). Buying an individual stock, to me, is putting all of my eggs in one basket; instead, I like to spread out my eggs to different companies and industries. Doing this on your own by purchasing hundreds or thousands of individual stocks would be extremely time-consuming, confusing, and potentially expensive, so instead of buying individual stocks, I like to buy baskets of stocks.

- **ETFs** (exchange-traded funds)—These are like baskets of stocks; by purchasing an ETF you can become part owner in hundreds or thousands of companies at once. They're usually passively managed (although you can get actively managed ones—those cost more, but are still typically less than mutual funds), meaning they don't have someone actively choosing what the fund is investing in each day. Depending on the strategy for the ETF, it has the potential to provide you with automatic diversification. Some ETFs concentrate on one industry (like banking, for example), or one country (like the US), which to me isn't diverse enough, so make sure you review the strategy for what you're buying before you consider investing in it.

Some people will buy a single ETF and that will be their entire portfolio; others might buy three: for example, a US ETF that holds the biggest and best companies in America, an international ETF that holds the biggest and best companies internationally, and a US bond ETF that holds bonds in America.

- **Mutual Funds**—These are typically sold by financial advisors and are generally the most expensive option of the bunch. They are like ETFs in the sense that they are baskets of stocks, they have different strategies, and you can also get ones that hold bonds, so it can be an entire portfolio in a single mutual fund. Essentially what happens with a mutual fund is that your money is pooled with that of other investors, and the fund manager uses the money to invest—they are actively choosing which investments the fund will be in. Some believe this active strategy can result in higher returns, but studies show this isn't the case—over a fifteen-year period, over 90 percent of actively managed funds failed to beat the market.[70]

This means you could have been better off investing in a passive investment like an ETF that tracked the overall market, because it would have had higher returns and lower fees (double win).

- **Index Funds**—These are similar to ETFs in the sense that they are passively managed (no fund manager actively picking the investments each day), and they're baskets of stocks. They track an index, which is just an indicator or measure of something, usually like a list. For example, there are index funds that track the S&P 500—all this means is that there is an index (a list) called the S&P 500, which is comprised of the five hundred biggest and best companies in America. An index fund that tracks the S&P 500 would just own a small piece of every company in the S&P 500—the strategy of the fund would be to replicate the list.

- **Target-Date Funds**—These are some of my favorites for people who are just starting to invest for retirement, because they're so simple. They're an entire portfolio in one, and they mitigate risk for you by putting you in less risky investments as you get older and closer to needing the money. This is an investment that you can purchase, keep putting money into, and really not have to worry about because it does all the work for you. It works to

---

70 businessinsider.com/personal-finance/investment-pros-cant-beat-the-stock-market-2020-7

maximize your returns when you're younger, and minimize risk when you're older!

- **Asset Allocation Funds**—These are newer investments, somewhat like ETFs but slightly more expensive. However, instead of having, for example, the three-ETF portfolio I described previously, you could buy an asset allocation fund that has everything in it that you need—like international stocks, US stocks, and even bonds. These can be thought of as an entire portfolio in one! Vanguard and iShares both have some well-liked options for these. The difference between an asset-allocated fund and a target-date fund is that, while the distribution (how much you own of stocks versus bonds) of assets (investments) changes to become less volatile (risky) as time goes on in a target-date fund, with an asset allocation fund, it does not. So if you invest in a fund that is 80 percent stocks and 20 percent bonds, it will always be that allocation (distribution). This means that if, in the future, you decide you'd like to have less stocks and more bonds (or vice versa), you'd have to sell your investments in this fund to reinvest in the new fund (this cannot be done automatically for you).

- **Bonds**—This is where you lend out your money to companies or the government and get paid interest. Bonds have the least opportunity for growth, but that's not what they're there for—you add bonds in your portfolio to mitigate risk. How do bonds mitigate risk? Bonds are what's known as fixed income, meaning that you know exactly what return you're getting before you sign up; it's fixed. The rates are typically lower than what you can get investing in the stock market, closer to 3–4 percent versus an average 7–10 percent for stocks, but they are used to provide some stability to your portfolio (the theory is you'll see less ups and downs in the short term when you have more bonds, but your overall return will likely be less than if you had more stocks or stock alternatives, like

ETFs). Usually, as you get closer to your goal date, you'd want to increase the number of bonds you hold in your portfolio to provide you with less volatility/changes to the value of your account (remember, stocks are volatile and unpredictable in the short term), and more stability.

There are two main types of bonds: government bonds (also known as treasury bonds) and corporate bonds.

> **Government bonds** (treasury bonds) are seen as more reliable, as you are lending your money through the bond to the government—and there is a very high probability that the *government* will pay you back. Because they're more reliable, and less risky, they typically provide lower returns than corporate bonds. Usually, government bonds are preferred to corporate bonds in a long-term diversified portfolio. Depending on the country you reside in, they may also have preferential tax treatment (meaning you may pay less in taxes on money you make from these bonds than from corporate bonds).

> **Corporate bonds** are a way you can lend your money to a business through a bond. These are more risky than government bonds because they depend on a company paying you back your money. There are different ratings of companies—the larger, more secure companies typically pay a lower interest rate or return (this is also known as a *coupon payment*) than smaller, less-established companies. Similar to the government bonds, this is because lower risk typically yields a lower return, and higher risk comes with a premium to entice investors.

You make money investing in a bond in two ways: first, by the interest (or coupon) payment. These are made to you periodically and paid out based on the specifics for the bond (e.g., twice a year, quarterly). The second way is by the borrower (company or government) repaying the money you gave to them. You can lose money in a bond if the borrower defaults on the loan (doesn't pay you back). With large, financially sound companies this is rare, and it is unheard of for governments.

You can invest in individual bonds (similar to individual stocks), or you can invest in a bond ETF. Bond ETFs differ from individual bonds in the sense that the ETF never "matures"—meaning the investor is not repaid the money they invested, rather it stays within the ETF and is reinvested in further bonds. Typically, bond ETFs are good for people who are looking to hold them long-term (not sell), who don't want that money sitting around in cash (because inflation eats it), but are okay with getting lower returns than from stocks. In the short term, bond ETFs can rise and fall in price based on what's happening with overall interest rates in the economy—they typically have an inverse relationship with interest rates, meaning if the government decides to raise interest rates, typically the price of bond ETFs will fall in the short term (when they lower interest rates, typically bond ETF prices rise). This is because the old bonds (and associated interest rates) become either more or less appealing to investors, and will thus change demand for the investment.

For example, if interest rates are rising, that means the bonds within the bond ETF are at the old, lower, interest rates. This means investors could theoretically make more money with a newer bond, because it would provide a higher interest rate. So in the short term, the demand for the bond ETF can fall.

GETTING INVESTED

So how do you buy these investments? You have three main options: 1) Financial advisor, 2) robo advisor, and 3) self-managed. When would you choose each?

Financial Advisor—I would choose a financial advisor if I was just getting started, if I was educated but still nervous about investing, and I was prone to making emotional decisions with my money. Sometimes it can be a good idea to start out with a financial advisor, get used to investing (maybe for six months to one year), and then look at moving your investments into something more cost-effective once you feel good about what investing is actually like. Other reasons to use a financial advisor could be to get assistance with a more complicated financial situation, or to help plan for things like taxes and retirement (they have special tools for this). The financial advisor works for or with a brokerage, and is then able to give you access to buy and sell investments this way.

Robo Advisor—A robo advisor is like a financial advisor, except it's a robot online and uses a questionnaire that you fill out about your personal financial situation and goals to recommend and then manage a portfolio for you. This can be a good intermediary for someone who doesn't want to pay for a financial advisor, is in control of their emotions when it comes to their money, and knows about investing, but doesn't want to be in total control of their portfolio. You may have limited ability to speak with a human if you choose this option, so make sure you do your research on what the company provides to their clients. The robo advisor is a brokerage that gives you access to buy and sell investments.

Self-Managed—This is the most cost-effective and can be the most involved if you decide to create your own portfolio (by choosing each one of your own investments), but it doesn't have to be. You can make it super complicated by trying to put together your own choice for winning stocks, or you can make it super easy and choose an investment type (like a target date fund or asset allocation fund) and let all the heavy lifting be done for you.

You can be a good investor choosing any of the above. Making money in the stock market overall is quite simple—all you need to do is buy and hold diversified investments like ETFs, index funds, asset allocation funds, or even a target date fund. Being good at investing doesn't mean finding the hottest company or stock; studies show that vanilla investing—boring investing, buying, holding, not getting emotional, being diversified/ not putting all your eggs in one basket, and not tinkering with your investments—is the best way to make money.

Historically speaking, it would be quite difficult to lose money by following that strategy. People don't lose money when the stock market crashes; they lose money when they strategize poorly, put all their eggs in one basket, invest for the short term, or make emotional decisions when it comes to investing. The stock market "crashing" doesn't mean you lose money, and in fact, stock market crashes are actually incredible times to invest more money (into the right diversified investments) because things are *on sale*.

Stock market crashes are normal. On average, stock market corrections happen once every 1.84 years. Does that mean that everyone who has invested in the stock market loses all their money once every 1.84 years? No—because there is a big difference between a paper loss and a real loss. A paper loss is when you lose money on paper; when the value of what you've bought goes down. The thing is, if you don't sell, it's not a real loss, and it doesn't mean anything (unless you are not properly diversified, your eggs are in one basket, or what you've invested in is no longer viable—for example, you bought stock in a single company and it's going bankrupt).[71]

Most people lose money in a stock market crash because they:

· Made bad decisions beforehand

· Get emotional and sell when the markets go down

---

71   fool.com/investing/2020/10/10/the-3-most-important-stock-market-crash-statistics/

- Are day-trading

- Aren't investing long-term

- Are overexposed in one industry, country, or company

- Aren't set up financially on the back end (don't have an emergency fund, have high-interest debts to pay, or *need* the money now)

Investors do not lose money simply because the stock market crashes. In fact, if we look at stock market history, the market has always recovered. So even when it crashes, it has always eventually come back up—this is why we can't time the market, and why we don't invest for short periods of time, but spend time in the market and invest for the long term. Even during the worst, the *absolute worst* twenty-year period falling between January 1973 and December 2016, the S&P 500 index still returned an average of 6.4 percent annually.[72]

S&P P 500 Historical Annual Returns (source: Investopedia)

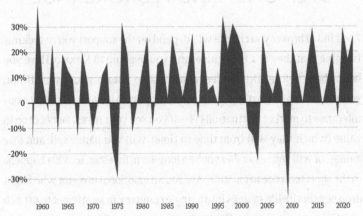

performance is calculated as the % change from the last trading day of each year from the last trading day of the previous year

---

72   thebalance.com/rolling-index-returns-4061795

If we know that stock market crashes are normal, we can start to expect them, and by expecting them, we can prepare ourselves emotionally and financially (by having our emergency fund in cash, investing for the long term, and having high-interest debts paid off). It's not whether a crash will happen, it's when. So when you see it occur, don't let it stress you out—because, even if you lose 50 percent of the value of your investments today, does the value today matter when you don't need the money for thirty-five years? You still hold the same number of investments, and as long as you are diversified properly, you'll be okay because the market as a whole has always recovered from a crash.

FOUR STEPS TO START INVESTING

Now that we have our background information down, let's talk about how you can get started investing, step by step.

STEP ONE: FIND A BROKERAGE

The kind of broker you choose will depend on the support you're seeking. Imagine that they're a tour guide, and you're going to Mexico. Have you been there before? Do you feel comfortable out on your own? If not, you may want to start out with more support. Ask yourself what your tolerance to market fluctuations is—if you see your investments drop in value (which they will from time to time), will you panic, sell, and lose money, or will you remember you're a long-term investor, so what happens in the short term doesn't matter? Are you an emotional investor who might drop your entire life savings into a single company in an attempt to *get rich quick*, or are you more methodical with your goals? Whether or not you use a financial advisor, you still need to learn everything you can about investing to ensure you are making good decisions. Most investors do the opposite of what you're supposed to do—they buy high (catch FOMO) and sell low (get scared). A financial advisor can stop you from making bad decisions; that's their real benefit (you can make the same portfolio on your own for very low cost).

Some clients like to start with an FA (financial advisor; that's how I started for about six months), then move on to either a robo advisor or self-directed account (where you do everything yourself). This will allow you to get experience investing but not have to pay out tons in fees over the years. Remember, a 1 percent difference in fees could mean ten years less in retirement income. Learning how to invest on your own is a great way to save money and have your money work harder for you. Also remember that your advisor is getting paid their fee whether you make money or not.

A robo advisor is a great option if you don't mind not having human help—it's super simple, you find one, answer a questionnaire, and then open your account/deposit your money; they do everything else. Robo advisors are more expensive than self-directed, but cheaper than a financial advisor. Remember, good investing isn't sexy, it's boring and vanilla—you put in your money, leave it alone, and then, in the long term, build a fat bank account. Want to get rich sooner? Invest more, don't take on riskier investments.

Some of my favorite brokerages are:

USA: TD Ameritrade, Charles Schwab, Vanguard (not Robinhood)

Canada: Wealthsimple, Questrade, TD Direct Investing

I like each of these brokerages for a few reasons, but it's mainly because they have good reputations and good customer service; many have options to work with a financial advisor if desired; some have robo advisors; they generally have low or no fees, with easy-to-use websites and apps; and they offer access to open tax-sheltered or tax-advantaged accounts (like your IRA in the US, or your TFSA or RRSP in Canada).

At the time of writing, Robinhood is not on the list of brokerages I would recommend—and is actually one I would personally steer clear of. The way the company and app are designed promotes short-term speculative investing—which is great when you're a company that receives a fee for every trade or transaction, but as our data shows, not great if you're trying to invest (not gamble). When we gamble with our savings, it can be a great way to *lose* money (and that's the opposite of what we're trying to do here). Not only does the infrastructure promote gambling-like trading, but they've also had loads of issues with customer service, and some shady business practices too.[73]

STEP TWO: OPEN YOUR ACCOUNT WITH YOUR BROKERAGE OR ADVISOR

The biggest expense you have in life is taxes, so we invest through tax-sheltered or deferred accounts when and where possible.

This means that, either the money you deposit into these accounts is tax-free (meaning you get to write off your deposit as an expense on your taxes, which could result in a tax return at year-end) and you pay the taxes upon withdrawal in the future (this is tax-deferred), or you get to grow your money and pay nothing in taxes on your gains (this is tax-sheltered).

---

73 nytimes.com/2020/07/08/technology/robinhood-risky-trading.html

Pro Tip: To get the full benefit of a tax-deferred account, the money you get as a tax refund should be reinvested as well—this way you get to supercharge your investments today and let that tax money work for you.

USA: Tax-sheltered accounts (the US has retirement accounts only that fall into this category)—401(k) and Roth 401(k) are through your employer only, while IRA and Roth IRA can be opened on your own. If you're trying to decide between a Roth and traditional accounts, you can try out different free online calculators to see what makes the most sense for your personal situation. These calculators have you input your personal financial numbers, like your income and the amount you're investing, and will use those to determine which account would provide you with the better return overall.

The difference between the two accounts is when you pay taxes (either up front with the Roth IRA, or later with the traditional IRA).

- **Roth IRA:** Pay taxes on your income today, but let your investments grow tax-free (you will not pay tax on the money when you withdraw it).

- **Traditional IRA:** get a tax write-off for the money you invest today (which means you can save money on your taxes, and potentially get a refund), but pay taxes on your investments when you withdraw them.

Generally, the Roth makes more sense for most people, but it depends on your personal financial situation—so always make sure to run your numbers first!

Canada: Tax-sheltered accounts—TFSA (tax-free savings account) used for any goal (no restrictions on taking out the money, whereas a retirement-specific account may restrict the reasons why you may withdraw, or when, for example at a certain age, or for a certain expense), or an RRSP (registered retirement savings plan) which is tax-deferred (you pay taxes when you withdraw the money, but get a tax write-off for your contributions today—similar to the traditional IRA). Your RRSP is used for retirement savings.

There are limits to what you can invest in each of these accounts—for example, an IRA and TFSA have annual contribution limits of $6,000, versus a 401(k) with a limit of $20,500 for 2022. So if you have maxed out your contributions (do that first if it makes sense for your goal) and want to invest more, your next step would be to open a taxable brokerage account (just a regular account with no tax advantages).

If you decide that your goals do not fit into any of the potential tax-sheltered or deferred accounts available to you, your next option is to use a simple brokerage account—which is nothing more than an account with no special tax treatment. Before opening a brokerage account, please ensure you understand that earnings will be taxed. Rates will vary based on your country and the length of time your investments are held in the account. I always recommend speaking with a tax professional prior to acting on your investment strategy to ensure you are set up in the most preferential way.

For example, if you are in the US, saving for a goal outside of retirement, you may want to invest through a brokerage account so there are no fees or penalties to withdraw the money.

It is usually a good idea to have a variety of accounts, as it's important to choose the best account for your situation based on your goal (retirement or other) and timeline for that goal (if you're seeking early retirement, you may want to have some of your investments in a standard taxable brokerage account so there are no restrictions on when you can remove your money, or fees/penalties imposed for doing so).

USA Example: Let's say that Sally has a 401(k) with an employer match. The 401(k) is known for having limited choices available for investment, and very high fees—so what would I do if I were Sally? Would I continue investing in the 401(k), or would I look for alternatives to combat the higher fees (even if that meant giving up the employer match)?

Personally, I would invest in the 401(k) to get the employer match (always take the free money, because hello, it's *free money*) and then open either an IRA or brokerage account, depending on her retirement goals, to invest the money above and beyond what I need to contribute for the employer match. This way, you get the free money from the employer match, but then save on fees and expenses by investing through your own accounts, where you have more control.[74]

STEP THREE: TRANSFER MONEY INTO YOUR NEW ACCOUNT

Remember Rule Two, where we talked about paying your future self first and automating your savings? We also want to automate our investments. To do this, you're going to set up automatic transfers (the ones we talked about in chapter 5) into the account each time you get paid, so you can take your brain out of it. The more you automate your finances, the more likely you are to be successful and not get in your own damn way.

Pro Tip: Make sure that you've set up your money to automatically invest when you transfer it (like with a robo advisor or financial advisor), or that once you transfer the money, you're making time to actually buy the investments when the money is in the account.

---

74 The same can be said for Canada with your RRSP if offered through your employer with a match.

How much do you invest? Work backward from your goal (reverse-engineer it, like we talked about in chapter 6). You're going to determine how much you need to save today to reach your goal in the future, along with your estimated rate of return (check historical returns to get an idea of the average past return for your investment), and use these numbers for your automatic transfers.

Pro Tip: Remember to make it a smart goal, so you know exactly what you need and when you need it—we don't want to be taking a hope, wish, pray approach to our investments!

Caveat: Historical returns do not promise future returns, but they're a good starting place. Remember: the more data you get the better your decision making will be.

STEP FOUR: INVEST THE MONEY & CHOOSE OUR INVESTMENTS

In Step Four, we are bringing it back to the rule of "invest early and often" from chapter 5.

Caveat: Remember, don't invest money you need in the next five years—it is risky, and the market is unpredictable in the short term. While capital growth is the goal (getting our money to grow and work for us), capital preservation is also key (not losing your money). We need to strike a delicate balance, growing our dollars and not losing them.

If you need the money in less than five years, I would consider putting it into something that has a more guaranteed return.

US Options: a certificate of deposit (CD), high-yield savings account (HYSA), or maybe even treasury bonds

Canadian Options: a guaranteed investment certificate (GIC), high-yield savings account (HYSA), or maybe even treasury bonds

Which option you select depends on your timeline for the goal and your tolerance of risk.

For example, when you put your money into individual bonds or CDs (or GICs in Canada), your money is locked in for a period of time. If you're considering one of these options, ask yourself if you're okay with locking your money away for that set time frame.

If you need something with more flexibility, that's where a high-yield savings account (HYSA) might come in. While we always want to maximize how much money we're making on our investments, we also want to make sure that the strategy overall works with our goal. So if that means getting a 2 percent return on your high-yield savings account instead of a 3 percent return on bonds because you need the money within the next three months, that's okay—because the overall parameters of the savings account made more sense.

You can invest in a CD, a GIC, a HYSA, and treasury bonds through a bank.

For goals that are more than five years out (such as retirement), that's where you can start thinking about stock market investments like index funds, exchange-traded funds (ETFs), stocks, target date funds, asset allocated funds, and mutual funds. I personally like index funds, exchange-traded funds, asset allocated funds, and target date funds, because they can provide automatic diversification.

Caveat: Just because an investment owns shares in more than one company doesn't mean it's properly diversified. You want to remember to diversify not only by company and industry, but by country and time as well (investing for the long term and putting in money periodically over time).

For example, if you were to invest in an exchange-traded fund (ETF) that owned shares (pieces of companies) in fifteen oil and gas companies in the United States, would you feel that is enough diversification for your total portfolio?

Let's compare this to an asset allocation fund that invests in 13,000 companies across industries like financial, technology, industrial, health care, energy, utilities, real estate, and telecommunications in places like the USA, Canada, Japan, United Kingdom, China, and France, and owns over 17,000 bonds.

The beauty of funds that provide automatic diversification is that it takes the brain work out of investing and allows you to build a lazy portfolio. The best kind of investing is plain, boring, and vanilla.

Remember, you only lose money on an investment if it's no longer viable (like the company has gone bankrupt—this is why we don't buy individual stocks), or if you sell while markets are down; over the long term, markets have always gone up as a whole.

FREQUENTLY ASKED QUESTIONS

1. **What investments should I choose if I'm saving up a down payment to buy a house?**
   First things first: We're going to treat this the same as any other goal we're investing for. That means we want to understand a few things, with the biggest factor being: when are you buying it? If this is a short-term purchase (within the next five years), then

investments like stocks are likely not a good choice, as we know they're volatile in the short term.

Something I hear from my students all the time is, "But, Nicole, it's a lot of money just sitting there. Shouldn't I be putting it into stocks so it can work for me?"

And listen, I get it—with the prices of homes nowadays, your down payment is likely a pretty large chunk of cash. And maybe you're thinking, *Well, if I diversify, doesn't that mean my investment is safe?*

While diversification is imperative to lessen the risk to your investments, the other factor you need to consider is timeline. If your goal is less than five years away, then no, I would not invest the money. But what if it's six or seven years down the line—does it automatically become safer?

Not necessarily. The longer you hold your investments for, the higher the probability you will make money (when you're properly diversified, as discussed earlier in this chapter), but as we saw in the Vanguard study, the threshold to get to a 0 percent chance of loss, based on their data, was twenty years. Although your risk lessened at the five- and ten-year marks, it wasn't until year twenty that the risk went to 0.

Ask yourself if you can change your timeline to buy if you invest it and the markets go down when you want it out,

For example, let's say you wanted to buy a house in six years, but at year six, the markets are down. Are you okay to wait until year seven, eight, nine, or more for them to recover before you buy?

To really work out the risk and benefit here, what I would recommend you do is figure out realistically how much money you could actually make off your down payment if you were to invest it, and then see if that amount of money is worth the risk of having to delay your purchase to wait out the recovery of the market.

Let's say you're saving and investing a thousand dollars a month for six years to save a down payment for your home purchase. At an average return rate of 7 percent, that means after six years you could have $88,559 in your investment account.

Of this $88,000, just a little over $16,000 would have been free money (the growth of your investments).

Is the $16,000 worth it to you to have to potentially delay your home purchase by months or years as you wait for the market to recover?

There's no right or wrong answer here—this is where personal finance gets personal.

If this is a shorter-term goal, i.e., around five years, likely your best bet is in a HYSA, GIC/CD, or potentially bonds.

Pro Tip: There is a strategy in Canada where you can filter your down payment through your RRSP to supercharge your money, and save on taxes (if you have the contribution room available in your RRSP).

What this would look like is saving your down payment, then utilizing the Home Buyers Plan RRSP option to deposit your down payment into your RRSP, and then withdrawing that money after the allowable time frame (ninety days) to use to buy your home.

This allows you to write off the total amount of the down payment, which can provide you with a hefty tax return that you can use to invest, or to help with things like closing costs on your purchase.

Make sure you confirm details of the program before you proceed with it, as they may change.

Caveat: This money needs to be paid back to your RRSP within fifteen years, so if you use this strategy, make sure you have the ability to pay it back into the account (and reinvest it), or you could be hit with taxes and fees.

Unfortunately, no similar strategy is allowed in the US right now.

2. **Can I invest my savings to grow them to pay off my debt?**

The number of times I get this question! Contrary to popular belief, investing does not necessarily create a stream of income today if you are just starting out, as your nest egg is likely to be smaller and needs time to grow. Typically we need to invest over the long term, as that's where we make money. When we are talking about stocks and similar investments, yes, it's possible to make money now, but it's risky (because markets are volatile in the short term).

I would not personally invest the money I need to pay off my debt—what if you need the money in the short term and markets are down, you lose the money, and then you have no money to pay your debt?

This is also why we do not invest our emergency fund—who knows what the markets will do in the short term? No one. It needs to stay as cash in your high-yield savings account.

Pro Tip: If you have a one-year emergency fund, you may choose to invest three to six months of it in a three-month GIC or CD to maximize your return, but I wouldn't do anything more/other than that, and wouldn't do it unless you have twelve months in your fund.

3. Why don't you buy individual stocks?

When you buy one company you are gambling—you are predicting and betting with money that this company will outperform the market as a whole. Why bet on one company when you can own the entire market via an asset allocation fund or index fund?

4. Should I buy an Asset Allocated Fund or Target Date Fund?

You buy these funds if you want to manage your own portfolio (portfolio just means all your investments)—they're lower-cost and a super easy way to get started. They're my preferred method for those starting out because they're vanilla and don't require a lot of effort or thought, but they still grow your money. It's a win/win.

A target date fund is specifically for retirement—it's a super easy way to invest in a hands-off way and get a portfolio that changes the portion of stocks versus bonds as you get closer to retiring. To invest in a target date fund, you simply choose the year that you are going to retire (i.e., year 2051) and you find a fund called "name, target date 2051"—it's that easy. There are some great providers of Target Date Funds, like Vanguard—you can search for the specific names on Google, then look them up with your brokerage. They're professionally managed, everything is done for you, and they're low-cost. They can be a *great* option for retirement and for someone who wants to be hands-off without paying a financial advisor a huge fee.

An asset allocated fund is an entire portfolio in one (stocks and bonds), it gives automatic diversification, provides stocks and bonds that are automatically rebalanced, and has low costs. The difference between this and the target date fund is that the target date is meant specifically for retirement, whereas this portfolio could be used for anything—retirement included.

Caveat: As your goals change, you may want to buy into a different fund with a different allocation of stocks and bonds.

Vanguard, for example, has a variety of funds that vary in "risk" according to the proportion of stocks they have (the more stocks, the higher the "risk"). They have funds with 100 percent stocks (I own this one); they have funds with 50/50 split, 80/20, 60/40, etc.

When it comes to risk and having more stocks in your portfolio, typically you want to take as much risk as you need to hit your goals and not more. You can look at the prior annual returns to get an idea of how the fund has performed over time (remember that past returns do not promise future returns).

5. **Don't I need to know more about swing trading, market cap, and like selling covered calls?**
   No—this is not necessary to investing. This lingo is confusing, and leans closer to gambling than actual investing. Remember, good investing is boring, and vanilla. When we talk about investing, getting rich slow and steady, the way we teach it, is very easy—you don't need that stuff to be successful.

   If you want to get started, but you're still feeling nervous or like you don't know enough, it's potentially just anxiety/fear. Sometimes we think we need more info, but that's actually analysis paralysis coming back in. Whether you choose an asset allocated fund, target date fund, or a financial advisor with mutual funds, you'll do fine. You need to just get out there and do it, get the experience.

Caveat: This is not to say to just jump into something without doing your research; this is to say that, after you've done your research, are comfortable with the understanding of each option, believe in each option, and know that the option aligns with your goals, then don't spend too much time deliberating over two investments that are inherently the same.

If you're super nervous, start with a financial advisor; then, when you feel comfortable, transfer your money out (this way you can get used to the markets, get help setting up your first portfolio, and then move the investments into something lower-cost to save money).

If you want to do it on your own, make sure you understand the market psychology—the investing part isn't hard; the psychology is. Start small while you get comfortable; you can try putting a hundred dollars into a diversified investment and see what it does, to see how you handle the ups and downs (from an emotional standpoint). If you freak out and sell at a loss, maybe you need a financial advisor to guide you.

Ask yourself this: If the market dropped by 50 percent tomorrow, what would I do? If you think you would panic-sell, use a financial advisor to help prevent you from making emotional decisions that could cost you money. If you would stay the course or buy more because you believe stocks are on sale, then maybe you can handle it on your own!

Caveat: Just because an investment is "on sale" doesn't mean it's a good buy. The same rules apply here—is it diversified? Are you holding for the long term? And so on.

The key here is just to start and not let your fear get in the way. Remember: The scarier thing is never investing and not being able to retire.

CHAPTER 10

FINAL **THOUGHTS**

When I started telling people they didn't need a budget to manage their money, the majority found the concept insanely intriguing because budgets never worked for them, some were scared by the idea of change because traditional advice was all they had ever known, and a select few thought that it was completely impossible.

The naysayers usually cite that:

1. Businesses use budgets to run their finances and it works great for them

2. It wouldn't be possible to be successful with money if you didn't assign everything to a specific predetermined category

To that I say, businesses use budgets because, for a business, finance is purely a numbers game. Money in versus money out. Businesses are not individuals with thoughts, feelings, emotions, and psychological histories. There are no underlying money beliefs, thoughts, dreams, or hopes for a business. No financial trauma to overcome and understand. No scarcity or lack. A business is an entity, not a person. Ignoring the psychological, mindset, and behavioral parts of money is the reason so many people are feeling stuck in their finances.

The idea of managing your money without a budget might seem scary to those who don't like to go against the grain, who like to take traditional advice at face value, and who don't like to question why we're doing what we're doing. But in my opinion, if budgeting hasn't worked for you (and it hasn't for the majority of people over the long term), continuing to force yourself to budget your money without considering another way of doing things is akin to Barbara at the office, who takes three hours to complete a task you can do in thirty minutes because "she's always done it this way." Just because something has always been done a certain way doesn't mean it's right, and doesn't mean it's the best or most effective way to get to a certain result—and fighting change doesn't move us forward, it just keeps us stuck.

The smartest and most successful people in life are not those who blindly follow traditional advice or rules; they're the ones who see a problem and are able to think critically about it. To pick apart what's not working, and get to the root cause—and then find another way. That's what this book is all about—seeing something that has been studied and proven not to work, watching myself and others fail time and time again, and understanding that *there had to be another way*.

The process I outline in this book has been used in my own life to help me go from struggling and $40,000 in debt with $0 in savings to a millionaire at thirty years old. It's also helped countless others change the way they view and use money, and in doing so, become able to see financial successes they never thought possible—all with ease, without feeling restricted, and without a budget.

In order to manage our money without a budget, we need to:

- Learn what the traditional advice is, or the prevailing wisdom when it comes to personal finance, and be able to pick apart the ways it's wrong or ineffective

- Understand the reasons why this advice has been passed down through the generations in our society, and why there's such an emphasis on it, so we can better understand the motivations behind keeping this way of thinking alive

- Learn the different options we can take instead of blindly following the prevailing wisdom about personal finance in our society

From there, once we've laid the groundwork and foundation, we can get into the details and actions we need to start taking to find a new way of doing things. This includes:

- Learning about behavior, psychology, and mindset, and how those things impact the results we have not only with money and personal finance, but also in our lives as a whole

- Uncovering the ways we are self-sabotaging our efforts with money without even realizing it, and understanding that, without digging deep into our behaviors, and internal money scripts and rules, we will continue down the same path, because it becomes a self-fulfilling prophecy

- Learning the importance of rewriting our internal money scripts, figuring out what our personal money scripts are, and starting to challenge them

After we started to change our way of thinking about money, and thinking about the ways we personally interact with money (and what we believe is possible for ourselves with money), then it was time to start teaching you the new basic money rules and theories that will change your actions with money.

These basic rules and theories included:

1. Living on less than you make, so you can prevent debt and promote financial health

2. Paying your future self first by setting aside savings automatically for your goals, instead of going into the future hoping, wishing, and praying that someday you'll have what you truly want in life

3. Learning what happiness really is and isn't, and being shown how to use this to determine how you can spend your money in ways that get you real happiness (because money is a tool that we use to build our dream lives)

4. Investing early and often because you can build real wealth with less money if you give your investments more time to grow

5. Planning for the unexpected, because life is unpredictable, yet we can always predict something unexpected will occur

6. Determining where your money will work hardest for you because it can work harder than you ever can, including compounding while you sleep

7. Incorporating the WPM (Why Pay More) principle into your life so you can effortlessly save more

By following these simple rules with your money, in addition to the foundation we laid by helping you change the way you think about and view money, you can begin to manage your money without feeling restricted, or using a budget. Many of our students find that they are effortlessly paying off debt, saving, and investing, while feeling good about what they're doing, in ways they had never been able to in the past. From there we showed you some of the major financial traps people fall into, and how to avoid them. These traps are the big ones that can have huge impacts on your success with money, like buying a car, buying a house, and planning for your wedding. We discussed ways your financial goals can be accelerated with the right partner, or can become more difficult to hit if your partner isn't on board with your money plan—in addition to ways to get on the same page and start thriving with your money, future, and relationship. Lastly, we showed you the sexy stuff—the way we build real wealth, and make money while we sleep; why saving isn't the solution to your problems, and that changing your financial future is actually so much easier than you think.

This book has aimed to provide you with tactics to help you start managing your money without a budget, and the foundational work to help change your behavior and mindset when it comes to personal finance and what is possible for you. Remember: Personal finance is 80 percent mindset and behavior and only 20 percent tactics—focusing on only the tactics and ignoring the groundwork pieces will be the reason you stay stuck. Not because it's too hard, or it's not possible for you, but because you're trying to build your house without laying the foundation.

Something else I think it's important to reiterate is that, for many of you, this book may be the first time you were exposed to any of these concepts. It's easy to see something one time and think it's too hard—but I need you to stop confusing your inexperience with inability. Just because something is new doesn't mean it's something you can't do. It just means it's new, and you need to give yourself time to develop the skill. I encourage you to reread the book, highlight pages, and take notes. Use the concepts to create your own personal financial plan and roadmap to success. If you're stuck at any part on your journey, come back to the book and review the chapter you're struggling with. Money is a skill—skills take time to master. It doesn't mean it's not possible; it just means you must find the way that works best for you in your personal situation.

There are three steps to changing your life:

1. Recognizing something needs to change

2. Gaining the knowledge to make the changes

3. Implementing the knowledge to see the changes

You've gone through Steps 1 and 2—don't phone it in here and not move to Step 3. I see too many people get to this point and allow themselves to self-sabotage by never implementing what they've learned. Don't be that person. Life is hard, but we get to choose our hard. We can continue going through life, hoping, wishing, and praying for a change, or we can choose to be ready, choose to take action, and choose who we want to be. Where you are right now doesn't have to be where you're going (I'm a prime example of that), but it will be, if you fail to show up for yourself and take action.

Make a promise to yourself today to hold yourself accountable. To show up and do the work because no one is coming to do it for you. You get to be good with money. You get to be successful. You get to live your dream life. You just need to take radical responsibility for your actions and *choose* the life you want. We have thousands of versions of ourselves living within us, and by choice we become one—who will you choose to be today?

GLOSSARY
OF TERMS

Paying Your Future Self First: Setting aside money for your goals before anything else.

Investing: Using your money to buy something with hopes of it going up in value or making you money (a.k.a. getting your money to work for you).

The Mindless Dilemma: Going through each day as if it's a new day, only to repeat the same day over and over again because we haven't actively chosen to change it.

Hoping, Wishing, Praying for a Change: The act of not working toward your goals, but hoping that maybe someday in the future you'll happen to reach them.

Complexity Bias: Our innate urge to prefer complicated explanations over simplistic ones, even if the complicated one is untrue.

Broke Questions: Focusing on details in your financial life that make no real difference to your overall success with money.

Wealthy Mindset Questions: The focus on questions, scenarios, and statements that have the ability to enact big changes in our lives from a financial perspective.

WPM: Why pay more—the theory that says, why pay more than you need to in order to gain a certain level of happiness, fulfillment, or utility?

Interest: Money that either gets paid to you when you're lending money out, or money you pay when you've borrowed money.

Emergency Fund: Six months of savings to take you through your *unchangeable* expenses. In an emergency situation (loss of job or income, unforeseen health problems, economic downturn, etc.), you need to be reducing your expenses to what is *mandatory*. Eating out and getting our nails done is not mandatory, and although that might suck to think about, it also makes saving your six months' worth of expenses *easier* because you do not need as much as you think. **Note:** Three months is *not* enough. Emergency funds can also be used for unexpected circumstances, like your car breaking down, but my advice is to also start a separate savings account for more immediate problems and save the emergency fund for actual emergencies.

Stock Market: A place where buyers and sellers can exchange investments.

Inflation: When the general cost of living and items purchased for living increases. An average rate is somewhere around 2–3 percent annually, but it fluctuates in each country.

Compound Interest: Interest earned on your investment added to your initial principal; you're making money on your interest, and therefore the amount of interest you are earning is compounded.

Stocks: Owning a share of a publicly traded company. A volatile investment, as you are not diversified (meaning "all of your eggs are in one basket"), and if something happens to that company, it's possible to lose all of your money.

ETF (Exchange Traded Fund): A combination of securities, such as stocks or bonds, that are traded on the stock exchange, allowing you to invest in hundreds or thousands of securities at a time, which lowers your risk by diversifying your portfolio. They are passively managed and usually just track a specific industry or collection of stocks.

Mutual Fund: Quite similar to an ETF. It is an actively managed fund, meaning someone decides actively which investments to be in. Can include stocks, bonds, and securities for a fully diversified portfolio, and you can choose which fund is best for you based on your goals and tolerance to risk. The goal of a mutual fund is to have the returns beat out the market averages through active management (someone reassessing the funds invested); however, data shows us this rarely happens. These are more expensive than ETFs.

MER (Management Expense Ratio): The amount of money you are charged (shown as a percentage) on an annual basis to own your investment. Mutual funds typically have the highest MERs. The MER has a big impact on the overall returns and success of your investment portfolio—we should aim to have lower MERs when and where possible.

Index Fund: Includes a mix of stocks, bonds, and securities. Quite similar to mutual funds, but the main difference is that they are usually passively managed—where mutual funds have an active fund manager who picks the investments for the fund, index funds follow a certain stock market index. For example, an index fund may follow the S&P 500, so they buy stocks in every company that makes up the S&P 500 (a specific index of companies, or an industry). The biggest difference is the fees: fees for index funds are typically lower, but this is because they are not actively managed. Index funds aim to match the returns of a specific index.

Index: In investing, an index is a list or collection of companies (basket of stocks) that tracks the performance of that specific list.

S&P 500: An index of the 500 most reliable, biggest, or best companies in America. The S&P 500 is an example of a stock market index.

Bonds: One of the most secure kinds of investment, essentially a loan to a corporation or government body with defined interest repayments. Usually the interest is much lower than what you can get with any of the other investments we talked about (with the exception of GICs/CDs, which are usually the lowest).

GICs (Canada)/CDs (USA): A guaranteed investment certificate, or certificate of deposit, that pays a defined amount over a set period of time (for example, three years). They are very secure, but yield low interest rates because of this. They can have a place in your investment portfolio for shorter-term goals (i.e., buying a house); if you're planning for retirement, then a different option may likely be better, as sometimes GIC/CD interest is thought to be lucky to keep up with inflation (under normal circumstances).

High-Interest (High-Yield) Savings Accounts: Savings accounts offered by a financial institution that give higher than average interest rates on savings, usually for a defined period of time as an incentive to bank with them.

Core Values: Fundamental beliefs that a person holds, that become their *why*, the reason why they choose to do some things and not do others. An example of core values could be family, health, wealth, or status.

SMART Goals: Specific, measurable, attainable, realistic, time-bound.

Net Worth: Assets minus liabilities, used as a measure to see where you are with your financial goals. This is an unbiased view of where you're at with your money. I recommend calculating this once every six months to a year to ensure this number is growing. Your net worth is not your self-worth. We compare our net worth to our previous net worth, not to anyone else's. The younger you are, the lower your net worth typically is.

Assets: Things you own that have financial value (e.g., house, car, cash on hand).

Liabilities: What you owe (student loans, car loans, mortgage, etc.).

Self-Sabotage: Getting in our own damn way—when we continue to do what we shouldn't do even when we know better.

Conscious Mind: The part of our brain that we use to actively think (the part we use when we are learning).

Unconscious Mind: The part of our brain where the majority of our day is spent—it houses our patterns and beliefs, and it uses our past experiences to keep us in the familiar (because familiar is easy and safe).

Confirmation Bias: Confirmation bias is active when we knowingly or unknowingly seek out information and situations that further reinforce what we already believe to be true.

Money Block: Negative subconscious beliefs about money that prevent us from achieving what we truly want in life.

Money Mindset: The way we think and feel about money, typically based on our past experiences from childhood.

Affirmation: Personal positive statements that affirm something as true.

Fixed Mindset: When you believe that who you have been, your personality, your intelligence, and the like, are what they are—and that there is no changing it. You see challenges as a direct reflection of yourself and your abilities.

Growth Mindset: When you know that our potential is unknown, and that, although everyone might not turn out to be Albert Einstein, everyone has the potential to learn and grow. You see your challenges as an opportunity to learn and become better.

Abundance Mindset: When your beliefs are positive and rooted in knowing that there is plenty for everyone (including you), whether this be money, happiness, or love.

Scarcity Mindset: When your beliefs are negative or self-limiting, believing that there is not enough, or will never be enough, money, happiness, or love.

Money Avoidance: Belief that money is bad or rooted in evil, that you don't need money to be happy: "I don't deserve money," "People who have money are corrupt," etc.

Money Worship: Belief that more money would solve all of one's problems.

Money Status: Belief that money is status and one should always seek to attain more to climb the socioeconomic ladder.

Money Vigilance: Being secretive about money; being a good saver, but usually with a scarcity mindset about money.

ACKNOWLEDGMENTS

One of my all-time favorite quotes is, "We have thousands of versions of ourselves, living *within* ourselves, and by choice we become one." I've been a lot of different people over the years, both personally and professionally, but my goal has always been to keep choosing to be a better version of me than I was yesterday.

If you had asked me who I would grow to become when I was a teenager, I promise you my answer would have been a stark contrast to the woman I am today. Not only is this due to an endless amount of personal work, development, and growth, but it's also because of the love and support I've received from the most amazing man in the world: my husband, Justin.

Justin, through everything, you've been the one person I could always count on. You're my rock, my best friend, and the best father to Liam and Zachary. Without your help, I would have never been able to devote the time necessary to growing our business that has helped change the lives of so many and given me the opportunity to write this book, a lifelong dream.

Mindset is so important—not just with personal finances but with life in general—and you, Justin, are someone who has helped me refine my outlook on life and redefine what was possible for me. You've always believed in me and been my biggest supporter—none of these achievements would have been possible without you by my side, reminding me I'm not alone and that I was made for so much more than what I thought.

Liam and Zachary, thank you for motivating me to stay the course on my goals, even when times got tough. It's because of you that I knew I had to not only use this knowledge to better our lives, but to help better the lives of others as well.

To my publisher, Mango Publishing, the best editor, Hugo, and the girl who made my dreams of becoming a published author a reality, Geena: thank you. There is a world of personal finance advice out there, and I know my approach to money is different than that of many traditional writers, so thank you for taking a chance on me. With your help and dedication, we're going to show people that there is another way to win with money *without* outdated BS . That money gets to be easy. That where they are now doesn't have to be where they're going. This is such an insanely beautiful thing, and I thank you for providing me the opportunity to do this.

Finally, thank you to the *No Budget Babe* community for getting to know me, trusting me, and allowing me into your lives. Thank you for showing up to support me and for learning how to use what I teach to show up and support yourselves. It is truly an honor to positively impact so many people and to hear from you all each day on how you're winning, how you're believing in yourselves, and how different your lives have become by acting on our tips, strategies, and methodologies. I can't wait to see all the big things you do after reading this book.

Money isn't everything, but everything takes money. Because of the incredible people I mentioned here, I have the opportunity to get my message out, and I have the ability to teach the world how to use money as a tool to build their dream lives, reach goals they never imagined, feel more confident with their finances and stop feeling restricted by traditional advice, and find happiness—real freaking happiness.

Money gets to be easy when we have the roadmap to success.

Let's go!

ABOUT THE **AUTHOR**

Nicole is a CEO, money coach, and financial literacy advocate who specializes in helping women in their twenties and thirties effortlessly manage their money and build bank accounts that never stop growing.

Nicole knew there had to be more to life than living in a perpetual cycle of having too much month left over at the end of her money, so with $0 in the bank, she got to work. She learned everything she could about personal finance and was able to go from broke as a joke ($40,000 in debt with $0 in savings) to a $500,000 net worth in her twenties (that has now grown to over $1,000,000 at thirty)[75]—and that's how *No Budget Babe* was born. Since then, Nicole has made it her mission to help teach other women how to take control of their finances, so they can finally start winning with money and living the lives of their dreams.

---

75 businessinsider.com/personal-finance/young-millionaire-financial-freedom-strategies-2021-6

Mango Publishing, established in 2014, publishes an eclectic list of books by diverse authors—both new and established voices—on topics ranging from business, personal growth, women's empowerment, LGBTQ+ studies, health, and spirituality to history, popular culture, time management, decluttering, lifestyle, mental wellness, aging, and sustainable living. We were recently named 2019 *and* 2020's #1 fastest-growing independent publisher by *Publishers Weekly*. Our success is driven by our main goal, which is to publish high-quality books that will entertain readers as well as make a positive difference in their lives.

Our readers are our most important resource; we value your input, suggestions, and ideas. We'd love to hear from you—after all, we are publishing books for you!

Please stay in touch with us and follow us at:

Facebook: Mango Publishing
Twitter: @MangoPublishing
Instagram: @MangoPublishing
LinkedIn: Mango Publishing
Pinterest: Mango Publishing
Newsletter: mangopublishinggroup.com/newsletter

Join us on Mango's journey to reinvent publishing, one book at a time.

CPSIA information can be obtained
at www.ICGtesting.com
Printed in the USA
JSHW031021230323
39345JS00003B/3